Fast Forward ▶▶

Functional Sk...

Information Communication Technology

(ICT) Level 1

Activity Workbook and

Revision Guide

Building for
14
to   19
the Future

By
Lorna Bointon

Qualiteach Education

2010

© Lorna Bointon, Qualiteach Education

ISBN: 978-0-9565731-0-0

Published by
Qualiteach Education
Unit 36, Westminster Chambers
7 Hunter Street
Chester
CH1 2HR

Tel. 0800 612 5438   E-mail: contact@qualiteach.co.uk   Web: www.qualiteach.co.uk

First Published   2010

Qualiteach Education

Credits

Author
Lorna Bointon

Editor
Richard Bointon

IMPORTANT

Contents

Section 1:   Identify the ICT requirements of a straightforward task   **1**

Use ICT to Plan and Organise Work   2

    1.1 Activities   7

Section 2:   Interact with and use ICT systems to meet requirements of a straightforward task in a familiar context   **9**

Use Software Applications   10

    2.1 Help Sheets   14

    2.1 Activities   15

Select and Use Interface Features   17

    2.2 Activities   21

Adjust System Settings   23

    2.3 Activities   24

Section 3:   Manage Information Storage   **25**

Work with Files and Folders   26

    3.1 Help Sheets   27

Work with Storage Devices   28

    3.1 Activities   29

    3.1 Practice Makes Perfect   30

Section 4:   Follow and demonstrate understanding of the need for safety and security practices   **31**

Password Security   32

Computer Viruses   33

    4.1 Activities   34

    4.2 Activities   35

Section 5:   Use search techniques to locate and select relevant information   **37**

The Internet   38

Search Techniques   39

Currency, Relevance and Bias and Copyright   40

    5.1 Help Sheets   41

    5.1 Activities   42

    5.2 Activities   43

    5.1/5.2 Practice Makes Perfect   44

Other Search Techniques   45

Section 6:   Select information from a variety of ICT sources for a straightforward task   **47**

Select Information   48

    6.1 Activities   49

    6.1 Practice Makes Perfect   50

Section 7: Enter, develop and refine information using appropriate software to meet the requirements of straightforward tasks — **51**

Apply Editing, Formatting and Layout Techniques — 52

    7.1a Help Sheets — 57

    7.1a Activities — 64

    7.1a Practice Makes Perfect — 65

Graphics — 66

    7.1b Help Sheets — 67

    7.1b Activities — 69

    7.1b Practice Makes Perfect — 70

Drawing Tools — 71

    7.1c Help Sheets — 72

    7.1c Activities — 74

    7.1c Practice Makes Perfect — 75

Presentations — 76

    7.1d Help Sheets — 77

    7.1d Activities — 79

    7.1d Practice Makes Perfect — 80

Section 8: Use appropriate software to meet requirements of straightforward data-handling task — **81**

Numerical Data — 82

    8.1 Help Sheets — 83

    8.1 Activities — 84

    8.1 Practice Makes Perfect — 85

Graphs and Charts — 86

    8.2 Help Sheets — 88

    8.2 Activities — 89

    8.2 Practice Makes Perfect — 90

Databases — 91

    8.3 Help Sheets — 92

    8.3 Activities — 93

    8.3 Practice Makes Perfect — 94

Enter, Search, Sort, Edit Data — 95

    8.4 Help Sheets — 97

    8.4 Activities — 102

    8.4 Practice Makes Perfect — 103

Section 9:   Use communications software to meet the requirements of a straightforward task   **105**

Use E-mail   106

     9.1 Help Sheets   107

     9.1 Activities   110

     9.1 Practice Makes Perfect   111

Stay Safe and Respect Others   112

     9.2 Activities   113

Section 10:   Combine information within a publication for a familiar audience and purpose   **115**

Output   116

     10.1 Help Sheets   117

Checking Techniques   118

     10.1/10.2 Activities   119

     10.1/10.2 Practice Makes Perfect   120

Section 11:   Evaluate own use of ICT tools   **121**

Evaluation Techniques   122

     11.1 Activities   123

Answers   125

Section 1 ▶

Using ICT

Plan

Identify the ICT requirements of a straightforward task

Use ICT to Plan and Organise Work

Before starting a task it is important to plan it thoroughly to ensure that everything works smoothly and efficiently.

For example, before going out to buy a mobile phone you might do the following to plan and organise the trip:

- Check prices on the Internet
- Ask friends for advice
- Work out whether a contract or pay as you go is best for you and your current circumstances
- Ensure you have enough money to travel into town and enough funds to buy the item

The same principles apply when planning and organising a task involving ICT. Tasks using ICT may include:

- Using a word processor or desktop publishing program to type an invitation to a party or create a poster to advertise an upcoming gig
- Using an email application, such as Outlook Express or web mail to enter names and addresses of friends into an email contact list
- Using an Excel spreadsheet to work out costs of a party or monthly budget for mobile phone use
- Using a PowerPoint presentation to create a slide show displaying your holiday photographs and videos

Before you start, the following queries will need answering:

- What is the task?
- What is the timescale (when will it be completed)?
- What are the costs (if any)?
- How many people are needed to complete the task?
- How can ICT help to plan and organise the task?

Once you have worked out what the task is and what is likely to be involved in terms of time, cost and other requirements, you can then decide how best ICT can benefit you in planning and organising the task. See below how ICT can help plan and organise straightforward tasks:

- Word processor: create a timetable, storyboard or a mind map
- Spreadsheet: work out costs and timescales or create a Gantt chart
- PowerPoint presentation: create hierarchical charts to show the priority of each part of the task

Timetable

A timetable displays the task name, the estimated day and time that the task will be completed and a column which can be ticked to indicate that the task is complete. See the example below of a timetable created to help plan and organise a party:

Hannah is organising an 18th birthday party for her brother Ryan. She needs to determine how many people she will invite and then find and work out costs of venue, catering and entertainment before sending out the invitations. The cost of sending the invitations must also be calculated as part of the planning stage. Hannah has allocated two mornings next week to complete the task.

Task	Day	ICT	Time	Task complete ✓	Notes
Decide on guest numbers	Monday		9-10	❐	Limit to personal friends and family
Find venue	Monday	Internet search Google maps	10-11	❐	Ensure venue is centrally located for all guests if possible
Find caterer and work out costs per head	Monday	Internet search and spreadsheet	11-12	❐	Find out if there are any dietary needs
Book entertainment	Tuesday	Internet search/add costs to spreadsheet	9 - 10	❐	
Make a guest list	Tuesday	Word table/database	10-11	❐	Keep to agreed limit
Send out invitations and directions	Tuesday	Word/email Online maps	11-12	❐	To minimise costs, email where possible.

Storyboard

A storyboard is a rough design or initial plan of a movie, project, newsletter or other media that requires a design, such as a website. In the example below, Hannah has created a storyboard to help plan the invitations that she will send out:

TITLE here

Guest Name:

Venue:

Date:

Information:

Photograph of Ryan here

Completed invitation:

Mind Map

A mind map is a visual way of showing the thought processes involved in planning a project (sometimes referred to as 'brainstorming') which helps to break down each part of a task in the form of routes radiating from the central idea/concept. See the example below:

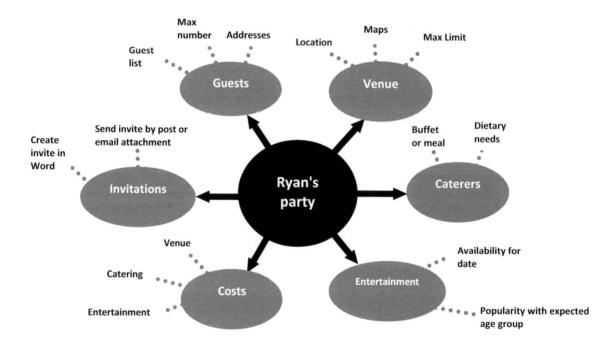

A mind map may also be a cloud or thought bubble with routes radiating from the central thought or concept. This method is supposed to aid creative thought.

© Lorna Bointon, Qualiteach Education 2010

Spreadsheet

A spreadsheet is a great tool to help you work out costs of a task. See the example below:

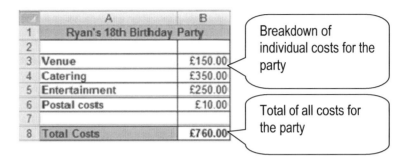

Gantt chart

A Gantt chart is a stacked horizontal bar chart, created using spreadsheet software, which shows the schedule of a small project, such as the task, the duration of the task and the hierarchy (order of priority or importance). The current status of a task is displayed along with start/end dates or times for the project. This helps the user to see the project's ongoing progression and development.

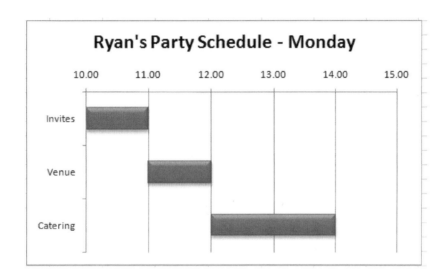

Hierarchical chart

A hierarchical chart is one that shows tasks or an organisation's workforce in order of importance or priority. See the example overleaf:

© Lorna Bointon, Qualiteach Education 2010

Ryan's Birthday Party

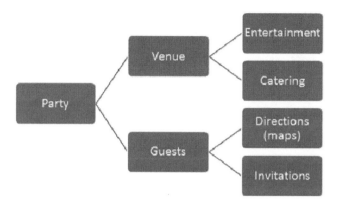

A hierarchical or organisation chart may also be used to indicate the hierarchy within an organisation, for example:

<table>
<tr><td colspan="3" align="center">Checklist:</td></tr>
</table>

Checklist:

- Task duration (how long will it take)?
- The software used – could other ICT tools make the task easier or quicker?
- Cost of project – some software is free to use or you can download for a specified period before buying
- Availability of ICT tools – is the chosen software easy to access?
- Output – consider the quality and effectiveness of the result. Could other ICT tools have performed the task more efficiently?

Match Makers

Match the planning methods with the correct descriptions below:

1.	Timetable		a.	Rough design
2.	Mind map		b.	Order of priority
3.	Hierarchical structure		c.	Timescale
4.	Storyboard		d.	Thought processes

Add your answers below (e.g. 1a etc):

1.		2.		3.		4.	

Choose a word from each of the boxes to correctly complete the sentences below:

timescale	storyboard	plan	spreadsheet	mind map

1. Before starting a task it is important to _____ it thoroughly beforehand

2. To ensure that a task is completed on time it is important to work to a _____

3. A _____ is a rough design or initial plan

4. A _____ is a visual way of showing the thought processes involved in planning a project

5. A _____ can help you work out costs of a task or project

As Easy As....

1. Which of the following is the most appropriate software for creating a Gantt chart?

A	Word processing	☐
B	Database	☐
C	Spreadsheet	☐
D	Web browser	☐

2. A spreadsheet is the most appropriate application for which of the following tasks?

A	Creating a budget for mobile phone usage	☐
B	Creating posters and invitations	☐
C	Creating play lists	☐
D	Editing photographs	☐

3. Which of the following statements best describes a hierarchical chart?

A	Displays levels of priority or importance	☐
B	Shows stages of creative thought processes	☐
C	Displays a rough design or blueprint	☐
D	Helps to work out costs of a task	☐

4. What type of planning tool does the image on the right represent?

A	Gantt Chart	☐
B	Mind Map	☐
C	Hierarchical chart	☐
D	Storyboard	☐

Section 2 ▸

Using ICT

Use

Interact with and use ICT systems to meet requirements of a straightforward task in a familiar context

Use Software Applications

Software applications are computer programs designed to perform a particular task. For example:

Word Processing Spreadsheets Presentations Database	**Application Software**
Graphics	**Picture/Photo Editing Software**
Internet	**Web Browser**
Email	**Communication Software**
Music/Audio Video	**Multi Media Software**

Application Software

Word Processing

Word processed documents include the following:

- Letters
- Posters
- Newsletters
- Memorandums
- Timetables

An example of word processing software is Microsoft ® Office Word 2007.

Spreadsheets

A spreadsheet may be used for the following:

- Budgets
- Accounts
- Sales
- Invoices
- Timescales
- Charts

ITEM	AMOUNT	PRICE	TOTAL
Peas	2	.45	.90
Beans	1	.59	.59
Sugar	1	.89	.89
Tea	1	1.79	1.79
Bread	3	1.20	3.60
			7.77

An example of spreadsheet software is Microsoft® Office Excel 2007.

Presentations

A presentation when it is running is called a slide show. A slide show has the following uses:

- Display products and services in a continuously looping slide show in a reception area
- Present an idea to your boss
- Present a talk to a large audience
- Show hierarchical structures

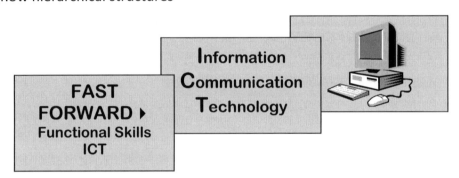

An example of presentation software is Microsoft ® Office PowerPoint 2007

Database

A database is an electronic filing system which enables the user to store data (such as friends' names and addresses) in a logical order. Examples of how a database may be used include:

- Storing and managing records
- Searching for specific records within a table
- Creating professional reports
- Using forms for data entry

An example of database software is Microsoft ® Office Access 2007

Web Browsing Software

Internet

The Internet is a network of interconnected computers which communicate globally with each other via an IP (Internet Protocol) Address. Using the Internet enables a user to access the World Wide Web (www). The World Wide Web is a collection of websites which are available on the Internet. Browsers include:

- Internet Explorer
- Netscape Navigator
- Mozilla Firefox
- Google Chrome

Communications Software

Email

Email software (Electronic Mail) provides a mailbox with an Inbox to receive mail. Users can receive, send, reply and forward mail with or without file attachments. Lists of friends' email addresses can be stored in a Contacts list. Users may use web mail which allows them access to their mail on any computer with Internet access wherever they are in the world. Email software includes:

- Microsoft® Outlook Express
- Microsoft® Outlook 2003/2007

Multi-media Software

Music

Music software allows a user to listen to music, purchase tracks and download them and make play lists of favourite mixes/tracks.

Video

Media software (media players) enable a user to download and view video. Most modern mobile phones and digital cameras have video capability, enabling video clips to be taken, with varying picture and sound quality, and then downloaded onto a computer.

Multi-media software includes:
- Apple QuickTime Player
- Apple iTunes
- Microsoft® Windows Media Player

Picture Editing Software

Photo Editing

Picture and photo editing software enables a user to edit, format and save pictures and photographs. Picture editing software includes:

- Adobe Photoshop
- Corel Paint Shop Pro
- Macromedia FireWorks
- CorelDraw Graphics

Checklist:

- ✓ Application software includes word processing, spreadsheets, databases, presentations
- ✓ Communications software includes e-mail
- ✓ Software that enables a user to browse the Internet is called a web browser
- ✓ Graphics software is used to edit and format pictures and photographs
- ✓ Multi-media software enables a user to download video and audio files

How to do it

To find out
how to do it,
follow the
instructions
below

Practical Exercise 1

1.   To open an application, select the **Start** menu

2.   Select **All Programs** ▶ and then the folder in which the program/application is stored (e.g. the **Microsoft Office** folder or the **iTunes** folder)

3.   Select the application from the sub-menu

The application may be saved on the desktop as an icon – if this is the case, just double click the application icon to launch the program.

QuickTime
Player

Match Makers

Match the software applications with the correct tasks below:

1.	Word processing		a.	Work out costs
2.	Presentation		b.	Create a poster
3.	Spreadsheets		c.	Add friends' details to a contact list
4.	Email		d.	Surf the Internet
5.	Picture editing		e.	Download audio and video
6.	Web browser		f.	Create a slide show
7.	Media Player		g.	Edit a photograph

Add your answers below (e.g. 1a etc):

1.	
2.	
3.	
4.	
5.	
6.	
7.	

1. Which of the following is the most appropriate software for storing data?

A	Word processing	☐
B	Database	☐
C	Presentation	☐
D	Web browser	☐

2. Which of the following can **not** be performed using music software applications?

A	Listen to music	☐
B	Purchase tracks	☐
C	Make play lists	☐
D	Browse the web	☐

3. Which of the following statements about Web mail is correct?

A	Enables access to e-mail on any computer with Internet access anywhere in the world	☐
B	Enables access on any computer, with or without Internet access anywhere in the world	☐
C	Enables a user to make play lists and download video content	☐
D	Enables a user to access e-mail on a specific computer in UK only	☐

4. Which of the following enables computers to communicate globally with each other?

A	An IP (Internet Protocol) address	☐
B	FTP (File Transfer Protocol)	☐
C	BPS (transfer rate of bits per second)	☐
D	An IP (Information Protocol) address	☐

Select and Use Interface Features

An interface is the front end of a program, such as the desktop in Microsoft Windows® XP or the screen on a mobile phone.

An ATM machine (Automatic Teller Machine or cash dispenser) also contains a user interface where the customer can press buttons on-screen or on a keypad to make transactions. Interface features include the following:

- Icons
- Windows
- Menus
- Dialog boxes
- Buttons
- Tool Bars/Ribbon
- Scroll Bars
- Zoom Bar
- Keypads
- Touch screens

Icons:

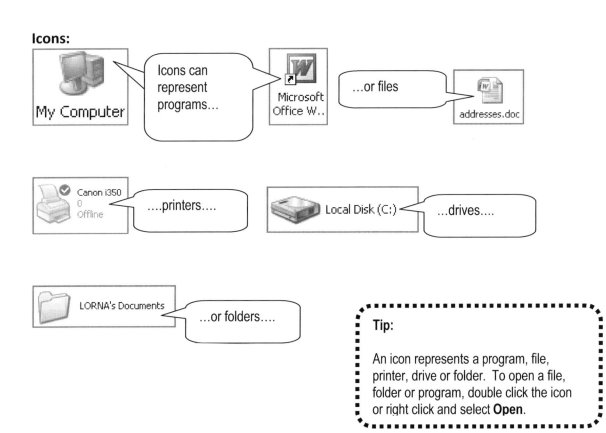

My Computer

Icons can represent programs...

Microsoft Office W..

...or files

addresses.doc

Canon i350
0
Offline

....printers....

Local Disk (C:)

...drives....

LORNA's Documents

...or folders....

Tip:

An icon represents a program, file, printer, drive or folder. To open a file, folder or program, double click the icon or right click and select **Open**.

Window

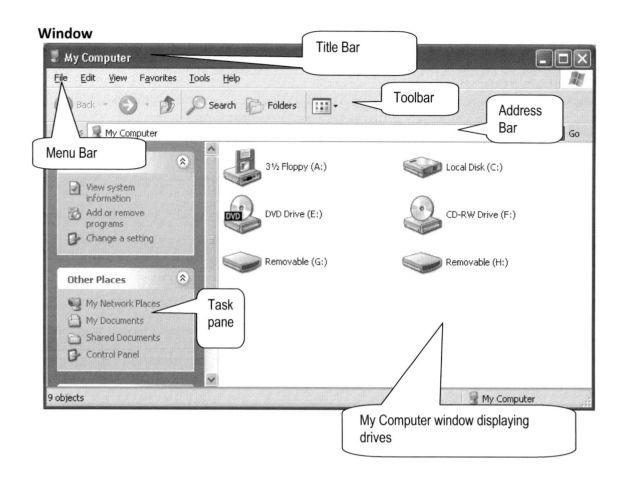

Title Bar

Toolbar

Address Bar

Menu Bar

Task pane

My Computer window displaying drives

Tip:

A window can be resized if needed. To resize, move the mouse pointer over the edge of the window and, when the mouse pointer turns into a double headed black arrow, drag to the required size.

Tip:

A window can be moved to another location on the screen. Point at the blue title bar at the top of the window and drag to the desired location.

Windows Buttons

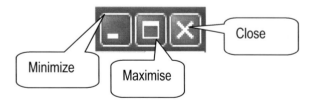

Minimize

Maximise

Close

Tip: When a window is maximised, the Maximise button turns into the *Restore* button. When clicked, the window is restored to its original size:

Scrollbars

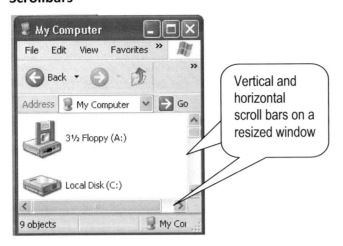

Vertical and horizontal scroll bars on a resized window

Tip:
The scroll bars will only appear when the window is resized and items within the window are obscured

Menus

Menu Bar: to close a menu without choosing an option, just click away from it

To open a menu, click the menu name. A line of dots.....displayed after a menu option indicates that a dialog box will be opened when the menu option is selected

A ▶ symbol beside a menu item indicates a sub-menu

Dialog Box

A dialog box enables the user to make further choices. To confirm an action in a dialog box, click OK or Close but to close a dialog without choosing an option, select the Cancel button.

Toolbar

Toolbar from the My Computer window

Tip:
Move the mouse arrow over the buttons on a toolbar to see a tag tip describing each button's function:

Ribbon

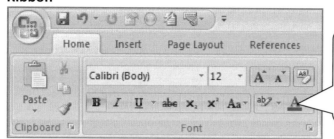

Office 2007 applications use a *ribbon* rather than toolbar and menus. A ribbon includes tabs containing grouped commands

Common to all Office 2007 applications:

The Office Button is a menu containing commonly used options, such as Open and Save:

The Quick Access Toolbar contains the Save and Undo/Redo buttons. Other buttons can be added as required:

Tabs replace menus:

Each tab contains a ribbon with grouped commands:

Some of the groups contain a Dialog Box Launcher icon which, when clicked, will open a dialog box:

Zoom Bar

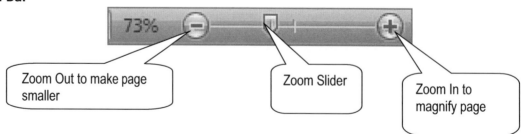

Zoom Out to make page smaller

Zoom Slider

Zoom In to magnify page

2.2 Activities

Match Makers

Match the correct descriptions to the icons shown below:

1.	Folder	a.	 Ryan's_party.xlsx Microsoft Office Excel W 12 KB
2.	Program	b.	
3.	File	c.	CD-RW Drive (F:)
4.	Drive	d.	iTunes

Enter your answers below:

1.		2.		3.		4.	

As Easy As....

1.   The Windows buttons do which of the following?

A	Enable a user to select formatting options	☐
B	Enable a user to print a document from the open window	☐
C	Enable a user to resize a window by minimising, restoring or maximising it.	☐
D	Enable a user to move a window to a different location on the screen	☐

2. The following statement describes which ICT feature?

The front end of a program, allowing a user to interact with a computer or other ICT device	

A	An Interface	☐
B	A motherboard	☐
C	A keyboard	☐
D	A mouse	☐

3. Scroll bars appear when…. ?

A	A window is maximised	☐
B	A window is minimised	☐
C	A window has been resized obscuring items	☐
D	A window is closed	☐

4. Which of the following statements best describes how to move a window?

A	Move the mouse pointer over the Title Bar and drag	☐
B	Move the mouse pointer over the edge of the window and drag	☐
C	Select the window, then select the Cut button, move to desired location and Paste	☐
D	Move the mouse pointer over an icon within the window and double click	☐

5. The following symbol ▸ appears after a menu option to indicate which of the following?

A	A dialog box will be opened when the menu option is selected	☐
B	A sub-menu will appear when the menu option is selected	☐
C	The menu option is already selected	☐
D	The menu option cannot be selected	☐

Adjust System Settings

Did You Know?

Increasing screen resolution maximises picture quality

A PC can be adjusted to suit a user's needs by changing the following system settings:

Picture quality/screen resolution: important when playing multi-media or games software to maximise picture quality **Desktop contrast:** can be adjusted to help users with visual impairment **Colour themes**: can be changed, so that the desktop, windows and other features are displayed in a different colour or formatted to display a picture (desktop)	
Icon size: can be increased to help users with visual impairment	
Clock: can be adjusted to display a different time or time zone **Calendar**: can be adjusted to display a different date or date format	
Mouse settings: can be adjusted to make it easier to see the mouse arrow; for example, make the mouse speed slower and apply a 'tail' so that the arrow can be seen clearly	
Volume: can be increased, decreased or muted as required	

Most of the system settings can be adjusted via the Control Panel:

2.3 Activities

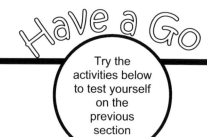

Try the activities below to test yourself on the previous section

Match Makers

Match the icons on the left with the correct descriptions below:

1.		a.	Change volume
2.		b.	Change icon size
3.		c.	Change the mouse pointer
4.		d.	Set the clock

Enter your answers below (e.g. 1a etc):

1.	
2.	
3.	
4.	

As Easy As....

1.   System settings can be adjusted from which window?

A	My Computer	☐
B	Windows Explorer	☐
C	Control Panel	☐
D	My Documents	☐

Section 3 ▶
Using ICT

Save

Manage Information Storage

Work with Files and Folders

A file is a document which has been created and saved on a computer, such as one of the following:

- A letter created using a word processing application
- A list of names and addresses stored in a database
- A monthly budget created using a spreadsheet
- A slide show created using presentation software

Saved files are represented by icons:

	A spreadsheet created and saved using Microsoft® Office Excel 2007		A document created and saved using Microsoft® Office Word 2007
	A presentation created and saved using Microsoft® Office PowerPoint 2007		A database created and saved using Microsoft® Office Access 2007

A file should be saved with an appropriate name to make it easier to locate and access. An example of a bad file name is **Doc 1**. This filename is not sufficiently descriptive and could relate to any file. A good filename is one that is descriptive, enabling the user to recognise and identify the file. A file is saved with a file extension to indicate the type of application in which it is saved:

- DOCX is the file extension for Microsoft® Office Word files
- XLSX is the file extension for Microsoft® Office Excel files
- ACCDB is the file extension for Microsoft® Office Access files
- PPTX is the file extension for Microsoft® Office PowerPoint files

A folder is used to store files. A folder can contain many sub-folders (a sub-folder is a folder within a folder). A folder system stores files in a logical way and makes them easier to find.

3 folders, the main folder is called **Music** and contains 2 further sub-folders, **Rock** in which to store rock tracks and **Indie** in which to store indie tracks

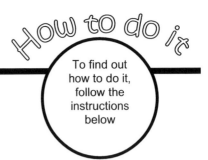

Create a new file

- Select the **Office Button** and then **New**
- Select **Blank ……** (document, workbook etc depending on the type of application you are using). Select **Create New**

Open a file

- Select the **Office Button** and then select **Open**
- From the **Look In** menu select the correct drive/folder in which the file is stored
- Select the file and click **Open**

! To open a file or folder from the My Computer window, double click the file or folder icon.

Save and close a file

Save

- Select the **Office Button** and then select **Save** (or click the **Save** button on the Quick Access Toolbar)

Save As

- Select the **Office Button** and then select **Save As**
- Ensure that the correct drive/folder is selected in the Save In box
- Enter a name in the **File name** box and click **Save**

- Select the **Office Button** and then select **Close**

Rename files and folders

- In My Computer, right click the file and choose **Rename**
- Enter the new name (ensure that a file retains the correct file extension)
- Press Enter or click away from the file

Delete files and folders

- Select the file or folder and then pres the **Delete** key on the keyboard
- Confirm deletion by clicking **Yes**

Copy and move files

- Select the file or files and then select **Copy** or **Move** from the **Edit** menu
- Select the correct drive or folder and then, from the **Edit** menu, select **Paste**

Create a folder

- From My Computer, select the **File** menu and then **New ▶ Folder** OR From the **Save As** dialog box, click the **Create New Folder** button
- Enter a folder name and press Enter or click away from the folder

Work with Storage Devices

Storage devices are devices on which you can save and store files and folders. A computer contains a hard drive, usually called the C: or Local Drive, which is built-in to the computer (although some hard drives can be installed externally). Other storage devices are removable and can be used to transfer data between computers or used as backing storage.

Backing up data is important in the event of disk or drive failure or fire, theft or corruption.

Hard drive	The hard drive stores the programs on the computer and is capable of storing a large amount of data	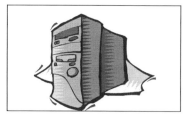
Floppy disk	A Floppy disk can hold up to 1.44 mb of data and is a removable storage device	
CD-RW	A CD-RW can hold up to 700 mb of data and is used to store data and audio files	
DVD-RW	A DVD-RW is used to hold film and movie files and can store up to 4.7 gb on a single sided, single layer DVD (can hold more if double sided, double layered)	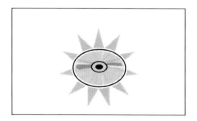
Memory stick	A memory stick is also referred to as a Flash Drive, USB Stick or Pen and can hold a variable amount of data measured in megabytes and gigabytes. This removable and portable device is inserted into a USB port to store and transfer data between computers	

Have a Go

Try the activities below to test yourself on the previous section

Match Makers

Match the correct answers with the questions below:

1.	A portable storage device which inserts into a USB port	a.	Floppy disk
2.	A removable storage device capable of storing up to 1.44mb of data	b.	CD-RW
3.	A removable storage device capable of storing up to 77mb of data or audio files	c.	Hard Drive
4.	This drive holds the programs on the computer	d.	Memory Stick

Enter your answers below (e.g. 1a etc):

1.		2.		3.		4.	

As Easy As....

1. Which of the following statements about file extensions is correct?

A	The file extension identifies the associated application in which the file was created	☐
B	A file extension makes it easier to locate the file at a later stage	☐
C	A file extension limits the amount of data capable of being stored in the file	☐
D	Adding a file extension is not necessary when renaming files – the file name is sufficient	☐

Practical Exercise 1

1.   Create a folder called **Party**

2.   Within the **Party** folder, create 2 further sub-folders named **Invites** and **Budget**

3.   Open Microsoft® Word and a new document. Save this document as **Guests.docx** within the **Invites** folder

4.   Close the **Guests** document. Open Microsoft® Excel and a new spreadsheet

5.   Save the spreadsheet as **Party_costs.xlsx** in the **Budget** folder

6.   Close **Party_costs.xlsx**

Practical Exercise 2

1.   Rename the **Invites** folder as **Invitations**

2.   Rename the **Guests** document as **Guest_list.docx**

3.   Copy the **Party_costs** spreadsheet into the **Invitations** folder

4.   Delete the **Party_costs** spreadsheet from the **Budget** folder

5.   Move the **Party_costs** spreadsheet from the **Invitations** folder into the **Budget** folder

Practical Exercise 3

1.   Open the **Guest_list** document from the **Invitations** folder

2.   Re-save the document as **Guests** into the **Invitations** folder so that there are two copies of the file with different files names

3.   Delete the **Guest_list** document from the **Invitations** folder

4.   Ensure that all files are closed

Section 4 ▶

Using ICT

Stay Safe

Follow and demonstrate understanding of the need for safety and security practices

Password Security

To log on to a computer on a secure network, such as in a school or training centre, you must log in with a username and password.

To withdraw cash from an ATM or to use online banking also requires a password in order to access the account (the password associated with a debit card or credit card is called a PIN or Personal Identification Number).

A password should be changed regularly and kept secret. It is important that you use a strong password. This means using random letters, symbols and numbers that cannot be easily guessed.

An example of a strong password: **TnJKL18$*@**

A weak password is one that can be easily guessed or 'cracked' by a fraudster. Examples of weak passwords are:

- Mother's maiden name
- Your date of birth
- Your birthplace
- Your name
- The word 'password'
- Using the top line on the keyboard (e.g. QWERTY or 123456)

Some organisations use passwords to gain access to specific parts of a network system. Authorised users are allowed to access areas on the system using their password (referred to as Access Rights) and this helps to keep confidential or sensitive data secure from unauthorised users.

Never give your password to anyone else. A bank will never ask you to give them your password, so do not reply to requests via email for your personal details or password. This is likely to be a scam called *phishing* which is used in identity theft.

Checklist:

- ✓ DO use a strong password made up of letters, numbers and symbols
- ✓ DO keep your password secret
- ✓ DO change the password regularly
- ✓ Do NOT respond to emails asking for your password
- ✓ Do NOT use personal information in a password that could be used to identify you

Document protection

Documents can also be protected by setting a password to open or modify the file.

- Select **Save As** from the **Office Button** and then, from the Save As dialog box, select the **Tools** button. Select **General Options** from the menu. Enter a password to open the file or a password to modify the file. Confirm the password and click OK. Select **Save** to save the file with password protection.

Computer Viruses

Viruses

A virus is a malicious threat designed to harm your computer and computer data.

To guard against viruses it is important to install anti-virus software and regularly scan your computer and drives for threats.

New viruses are being created every day which is why it is important to update your anti-virus software regularly.

Examples of anti-virus software are:

- Norton AntiVirus
- McAfee Antivirus
- AVG
- Kapersky Antivirus Security

Anti-virus software will scan your computer for threats and then either quarantine potential threats for later deletion or remove them (*disinfect*). There are many computer threats that can harm your computer; collectively they are referred to as 'malware' or malicious software. A *firewall* should also be installed to prevent unauthorised access to a computer system (called *hacking*).

Trojan Horses

A Trojan Horse is malicious software that is hidden so that it appears safe but allows a hacker unauthorised remote access to a user's computer. Trojan Horses can be downloaded unwittingly whilst downloading software or downloading ActiveX content from a website or via email attachments and can be used in identity theft.

Worms

A worm is a self replicating virus that can be downloaded and then passed on to other users via email attachments or network connections.

Spyware

Spyware is malicious software downloaded onto a user's computer which is used to monitor keystrokes and web browsing activities of the user. Anti-Spyware software should be installed to prevent spyware being downloaded onto a user's computer.

Adware

Adware refers to a program that displays advertising on a user's computer, usually in the form of 'pop-ups'. Adware advertising is designed to target the user based on results from spyware monitoring of a user's web browsing habits.

4.1 Activities

Have a Go

Try the activities below to test yourself on the previous section

Match Makers

Match the correct answers with the questions below:

1.	A date of birth or mother's maiden name is considered what type of password?	a. Phishing
2.	A random mix of letters, symbols and numbers is considered to be what type of password?	b. Changed regularly
3.	Fraudulently gaining personal data via a false request from a bank or other reputable organisation for identity theft is called?	c. A Strong Password
4.	To maintain password security, the password should be...?	d. A Weak Password

Enter your answers below:

1.		2.		3.		4.	

As Easy As....

1. A password used to access a debit or credit card in an ATM machine is called a PIN – what does PIN stand for?

A	Personal Indemnity Number	☐
B	Personal Identification Number	☐
C	Private Identification Number	☐
D	Personal Identity Notification	☐

Match Makers

Match the correct answers with the questions below:

1.	Malicious software designed to track a user's keystrokes and web browsing activities?	a.	Worm
2.	Malicious software designed to replicate via email attachments or network connections?	b.	Spyware
3.	Malicious software that is disguised as something safe but can allow a hacker unauthorised access to a user's computer?	c.	Firewall
4.	This should be installed to prevent unauthorised access to your computer?	d.	Trojan Horse

Enter your answers below:

1.		2.		3.		4.	

As Easy As....

1. How can a user ensure that **new** computer threats are identified and removed?

A	By regularly updating anti-virus software	☐
B	By installing more than one anti-virus software application	☐
C	By scanning for viruses every couple of months	☐
D	By using a strong password to access the computer system	☐

Section 5 ▶

Find

Use search techniques to locate and select relevant information

The Internet

World Wide Web

The Internet is a vast collection of computers that are connected via their IP (Internet Protocol) addresses over a global network.

The World Wide Web is a collection of web sites which can be accessed via the Internet. A web site contains one or more web pages which are linked together. The start page in a website is called a Home Page. To gain access to the Internet, a user must have the following:

- Computer
- Telephone line
- Modem or router
- Web browser software (e.g. Microsoft® Internet Explorer, Mozilla Firefox etc)

An ISP (Internet Service Provider) provides Internet connection for a fee. There are many ISPs available, such as BT, AOL, Talk Talk and many others, all providing connectivity services at differing prices and Internet speeds. There are different types of Internet connection:

- Broadband – this is always on and allows usage of the telephone line at the same time as using the Internet. The user pays a monthly fee for connection and may be limited to a specified monthly download usage.
- Dial-up – the user loses access to the telephone line whilst using the Internet. An advantage is that the user is only charged when the Internet is accessed.
- WIFI – a wireless connection that enables connectivity to the Internet via a portable device, such as a laptop or mobile phone. WIFI exists in 'hotspots' in public places such as shopping centres, restaurants and airports and is a convenient way of gaining access to the Internet whilst on the move.
- Pay As You Go – this is a pre-paid Internet connection using a Dongle (an adapter which looks similar to a USB memory stick) which is inserted into a USB port in the computer.

Search Engines

A specific web address is called a URL (Uniform Resource Locator) which is entered into the Address Bar to find a specific website. If you do not have access to the specific URL of a website you will need to use a search engine. A search engine is an Internet search tool which is designed to search within its vast database for specified keywords or phrases (called search criteria) entered by a user into a search engine box. A list of web page links that match the keywords, in order of relevance, will be displayed. When clicked, a webpage link will open a webpage which contains one or more of the keywords. A website designer will enter Meta tags which are descriptive words designed to ensure that the website is found.

Search Techniques

Did You Know?

AND, OR and NOT are called Boolean Operators

Advanced Search Techniques

Search engines use a database to hold vast amounts of information which can be queried by entering keywords into a search engine box.

For example, entering *cat* into a search engine will result in many web pages containing this keyword being found. To refine or narrow down a search, a user can do the following:

- Use specific keywords – e.g. Korat (type of cat)
- Use quotation marks – e.g. "Korat cat"
- Use advanced search techniques, such as + (AND), - (NOT), OR. Excluding words can be an effective way of narrowing down a search, for example excluding the word *Thailand* from the search (Korat –Thailand) will find web pages relating to Korat cats and not the city in Thailand.

Other search techniques include using the Advanced Search facility in a search engine, such as Google, to do the following:

- Enter an exact word or phrase
- Change the result of searches per page
- Specify a language and/or region
- Specify a file type (some websites are formatted as PDF)
- Search within a specific site (e.g. YouTube)
- Specify a date that the website was last updated
- Specify usage rights (e.g. free to use and share)
- Specify where the keywords show up (in the text on the webpage or the title, URL etc)
- Specify a numeric range (e.g. from £2000 to £5000)

For example, you may search for a car in the following way:

- Specify a make of car, e.g. Fiat
- Exclude words, e.g. Panda
- Specify a date that the page was last updated (within last week or 24 hours)
- Specify the region as UK with English as the language
- Specify a numeric range (e.g. only show cars between £800 and £1500)

The webpage link can be saved, so that it can be accessed later, by adding the page to **Favorites**. This is called *book marking* a web page.

Currency, Relevance, Bias and Copyright

Currency

It is important that information is up-to-date and current. To check the currency of information, always look for a date that the website was last updated.

To ensure that only up-to-date websites are found and listed, use an advanced search to select a timeframe in which the website was last updated (last 24 hours, last week etc).

Relevance

Keywords entered into a search engine may result in many web pages being found. Some of the web pages may contain the keyword but may not be relevant to your search. For example, entering 'hotspot' into a search engine may result in pages relating to WIFI hotspots being found but also pages on holiday hotspots or geological hotspots.

Bias

Bias is a one-sided opinion or view which may contain prejudice and not be based on fact. To gain a balanced view of a topic, it is important to check that information is not presented entirely from one point of view. Be careful about using wiki sites, such as Wikipedia, without cross-referencing with other sites of information as wikis are edited directly from a users computer.

Copyright ©

Some sources of information are subject to Copyright law which safeguards the copyright owner's interests. Copyright law ensures that text, audio, video, music, song lyrics or images belonging to the copyright owner (usually the creator/writer or publisher) cannot be copied without the copyright owner's consent. Copyright of literary, artistic and musical work lasts for 70 years from the death of a known author or 70 years from creation of the work, if the author is unknown. Check for copyright by looking for the following symbol © and any copyright information that has been provided on the website. If in doubt contact the copyright owner for permission. Unauthorised copying and sharing of text, images or music is illegal. Copyright law also relates to computer software programs and a licence is required before copyrighted software can be installed.

Plagiarism means passing off someone else's work as your own. Always get permission first before copying or downloading text, images or music and acknowledge sources of information.

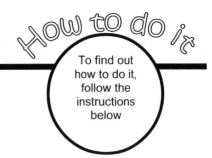

To find out
how to do it,
follow the
instructions
below

Access the Internet

- Select the **Start** button and **All Programs** (unless displayed in the Start menu) and then select **Microsoft® Internet Explorer** or double click the icon on the desktop.

Internet
Explorer

Enter a URL

- Click the cursor into the Address Bar at the top of the web page and enter the URL:

http://www.google.co.uk/

- For example, to access the Google™ UK search engine, enter:

All web addresses or URLs
start with Http:// (stands for
HyperText Transfer Protocol
and this is entered
automatically)

http://www.google.co.uk

World Wide Web

The domain name and
geographical location

- Press Enter or click the green arrow to go to the URL or click the X to stop the page from downloading.

Use a Search Engine

- Click the cursor into the search box and enter the search criteria, i.e. keyword or phrase.
- Press the Enter key or click the **Search** button (if using Google™ UK, click **Google Search**).

- A list of web pages will be displayed in order of relevance. Click a link to see the web page.
- Click **Advanced Search** to refine your search further. Advanced Search

Bookmark a webpage

- Select the **Add to Favorites** button and then select **Add to Favorites** from the menu.
- The **Add to Favorites** dialog box appears. Enter a name or keep the existing name and click **Add.**
- To see a list of stored web page links, select the **Favorites Center** button
- Click a Favorite link to open the web page Functional skills standards

Try the activities below to test yourself on the previous section

Match Makers

Match the correct answers with the questions below:

1.	A web address is called a ....?	a.	WIFI
2.	A tool which enables a user to search the Internet using keywords?	b.	URL
3.	A wireless Internet connection found in public places enabling connectivity via portable devices?	c.	Broadband
4.	This type of Internet connection is 'always on' allowing use of the telephone line whilst searching the Web?	d.	Search engine

Enter your answers below:

1.		2.		3.		4.	

As Easy As....

1.   To narrow down a search, the keyword should be enclosed within ....?

A	Curly brackets { }	☐
B	Round brackets ( )	☐
C	Square brackets [ ]	☐
D	Quotation marks " "	☐

5.2 Activities

Try the activities below to test yourself on the previous section

Match Makers

Match the correct answers with the questions below:

1.	Checking for currency means checking for...?	a.	Copyright
2.	This is a one-sided view or opinion which may not be based on fact?	b.	Plagiarism
3.	This law protects the rights of authors and publishers?	c.	The date that the web page was last updated
4.	Passing off someone else's work as your own is called...?	d.	Bias

Enter your answers below:

1.		2.		3.		4.	

As Easy As....

1. Copyright lasts for how many years after the death of a known author?

A	75	☐
B	60	☐
C	70	☐
D	50	☐

Practical Exercise 1

1. Access the Internet and enter the URL **www.google.co.uk** in the Address Bar.

2. Using the Google UK search engine find information on mobile phone apps, using the keywords **mobile phone apps**.

3. Refine the search further by selecting the **Advanced Search** link.

4. Ensure that the keyword **iPhone** is excluded from the search.

5. Ensure that the search will only show pages that have been updated in the last week.

6. Ensure that the search will only find UK web pages using the English language.

Practical Exercise 2

1. Using a Google search engine, perform another search to find information on web browsers. Refine the search by doing the following:

   o Exclude the keywords Internet Explorer (enclose "Internet Explorer" in quotes otherwise the individual word Internet and the word Explorer will be excluded rather than the complete string)

   o Search UK only

   o Ensure that web page information was updated within the last month

   o Find a page that provides information on Mozilla web browsers and save this page to Favorites.

Practical Exercise 3

1. Go to **en.wikipedia.org** and use the internal search engine to find information on *Dongles*

2. Check to see when the page was last modified or updated

3. Check for information about copyright (Terms of Use)

4. Check that the information is relevant (we want information on mobile pay as you go broadband usage).

5. Use a search engine to find another source of information about dongles.

6. Find a relevant webpage and bookmark it.

Important: to provide proof of Internet searches, and other tasks which cannot be printed normally, you will need to create screen prints: press the **Print Screen** key (to copy the whole screen) or the **Alt** key and the **Print Screen** key together (to copy a dialog box). Paste the screen print in a Microsoft Word document and save.

Other Search Techniques

Finding information

Keywords within Web pages can be located using the Find facility. Similarly, searches can be made using software applications, such as Microsoft® Word, Access or Excel. This can be achieved by using the find facility in Microsoft® Office applications.

Microsoft® Office applications

The **Find** tool is common to each of the Microsoft® Office applications and is used to find part or whole words or phrases within a document.

- Open a Microsoft® Office application, e.g. Microsoft® Word, Microsoft® Excel, Microsoft® PowerPoint or Microsoft® Access
- Select the **Home** tab and then, from the **Editing** group, select the **Find** command
- Enter the search criteria into the **Find What** box and click **Find Next**. Continue clicking **Find Next** until each occurrence of the search word has been located

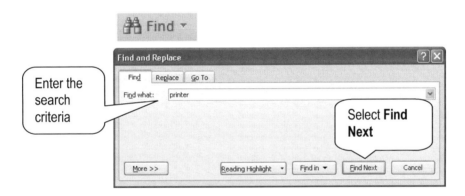

Enter the search criteria

Select **Find Next**

Microsoft® Internet Explorer

- Select the **Edit** menu and then select **Find on this page** (if the menu bar is missing, hold down the **Alt** key)

- Enter the search criteria within the **Find** box and click **Find Next**. Continue clicking **Next** until each occurrence of the search word has been found

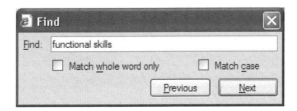

Section 6 ▶

Finding and Selecting Information

Select

Select information from a variety of ICT sources for a straightforward task

Select Information

Information Sources

Although the Internet is an easy to access and varied source of information, there are many other non-ICT based information sources available:

Non-ICT Information Sources
- Newspapers, magazines, books
- Images, diagrams, maps
- Conversations, text messages

ICT Information sources:
- CDs and DVDs (encyclopaedias, documentaries, language courses)
- Websites such as wikis, podcasts, weblogs (blogs), web-based reference sites (webopaedias)

Information sources, such as magazines, research the needs of the intended audience (an 'intended audience' is the user, reader or viewer) in order to target the correct age group/gender/interests.

Newspapers and Magazines: newspapers are daily and aimed at a wide range of people. Magazines may be published weekly or monthly and are aimed at a specific age group/gender or subject interest (e.g. gardening, model aeroplanes, computing). Both newspapers and magazines use headlines and/or images to gain attention and interest of the reader.

Websites: Websites can be a rich and varied source of information with web-based reference sites and online encyclopaedias and wiki sites. Wikis, such as Wikipedia®, are online encyclopaedias containing information contributed by other users. Information can be edited, e.g. added to or updated, directly from a user's web browser. For this reason it is important to use information from this source with caution as it may contain bias or prejudice or may not be accurate or based entirely on fact. Web logs (blogs for short) are web diaries which may also contain biased views and personal opinions. A podcast is a pre-recorded audio program which is available on a website to be downloaded onto a user's computer, iPod or other mobile device.

CDs and DVDs: Encyclopaedias, such as Encyclopaedia Britannica and other educational resources, e.g. language, learn to drive or computing courses are available on CD-ROM and DVD-ROM. Many other sources of information can be found on DVDs, such as documentaries on natural history.

Talking: Friends and acquaintances can be a valuable source of information and advice. Chatting directly to friends or via texting or email can provide information and advice; it can also help you learn from the experiences of others.

Match Makers

Match the correct answers with the questions below:

1.	A pre-recorded audio program that can be downloaded onto a mobile device?	a.	Newspaper
2.	A web log or blog is a ....?	b.	Podcast
3.	This is a non-ICT information source?	c.	Wiki
4.	On which type of site can information be updated directly from a user's Web browser?	d.	Online diary

Enter your answers below:

1.		2.		3.		4.	

As Easy As....

1. Which of the following is a non-ICT information source?

A	Podcast	☐
B	Blog	☐
C	Wiki	☐
D	Library book	☐

2. Wikipedia® is an example of which type of information source?

A	Online encyclopaedia	☐
B	Web log	☐
C	Educational DVD-ROM	☐
D	Pre-recorded audio program	☐

Practical Exercise 1

1. Access the Internet and find information on copyright law using an online encyclopaedia site.

2. Check when the website was last updated.

3. Check whether the site is a wiki site.

4. Cross reference the information you have found against another source of information.

5. On a piece of paper, write down the website addresses of the sites you visit.

Practical Exercise 2

1. Go to a site which provides podcasts (e.g. www.bbc.co.uk/podcasts).

2. Download a podcast of interest to you onto your computer.

3. Go to a site which provides web logs (blogs) such as www.bbc.co.uk/blogs.

4. Go to the BBC Internet blog on the BBC website.

5. Find information about subscribing to RSS blog feeds on the BBC website (if this information is no longer available on the BBC site, use a Google search to find any web page containing information on RSS feeds).

6. On a piece of paper, write down the website addresses of the sites you visit.

Practical Exercise 3

1. Visit your local library and find information on using the Internet and the World Wide Web.

2. Visit a book store and check out the DVD-ROM educational resources. Try and find information about using any of the Microsoft® Office applications on PC DVD-ROM.

3. Write down how easy or hard it was to find information from the different sources.

Note: for the practice assessments and the actual exam, you will be supplied with a source record sheet on which to record sources of information, such as website addresses.

Section 7 ▶

Developing, Presenting and Communicating Information

Edit

Enter, develop and refine information using appropriate software to meet the requirements of straightforward tasks

Apply Editing, Formatting and Layout Techniques

Information may come from many sources, such as:

- Email messages
- Letters
- Online forms
- Web pages

In order to enhance the appearance and presentation of information editing techniques can be applied to make it more readable and 'user friendly'.

Editing includes inserting or deleting characters or words, overtyping existing text or copying or moving information within the same or between multiple documents. An item of data which appears many times within a document can be replaced by alternative text throughout the document. If you make a mistake the undo and redo buttons can be used to undo or redo the last action you made.

Accuracy is important in a finished document and it is vital that text is checked for errors before it is presented on-screen or as printed output. The spell check facility in Microsoft® Office applications should be used to check and correct spelling errors.

Applying formatting techniques, such as changing the font, font size and colour can help improve the appearance of information and ensure that it is presented professionally.

Different types of information will require different formatting techniques. For example, a poster may require large font sizes and lots of colour, whilst a letter or business report will require consistent fonts and sizes throughout the document.

To enhance information, the following formatting techniques may be applied:

FONT TYPES/font types/**FONT TYPES**

FONT SIZES/SIZES

Font STYLE (**bold**, _italics_, <u>underline</u>)

FONT COLOUR

Font types, sizes, styles and colour should be applied to enhance information to make it more readable or to make it stand out. In a poster, a variety of fonts, colours and sizes may be used to grab attention. In a business document, a consistent approach to formatting is best for a professional appearance.

There are a variety of different fonts and sizes available from which to choose. Serif fonts, such as Times New Roman, have 'tails' on the characters (T) whereas a sans serif font (such as Arial) is plain (T) without 'tails'. Sans is French for 'without'.

WordArt is decorative text which can be used to enhance headings

• **Bullets** **and** 1. **Numbering**	• Bullets and numbering are used for enhancing and defining lists. A bullet can be formatted to display a different shape, colour or picture. a) A numbered list may be formatted in a variety of number formats, such as 1, 2, 3 or Roman numerals i, ii, iii, or letters a, b, c etc.
Alignment	Information may be aligned left, centre, right or justified. The default alignment for Office applications is *Left* aligned. This text is ***left*** aligned, which means that the left edge of the text is straight and the right edge is ragged This text is ***justified*** which means that both edges of text are straight <div align="center">This text is ***centred***</div> <div align="right">This text is ***right*** aligned</div>
Tabs	Tabs are parallel columns set at specified positions called tab stops on the page. Tabs can be aligned left, right, centred or aligned to a decimal point. **Item** **Price** Mouse …………………… 9.99 Keyboard……………… 14.99
Line spacing	Line spacing is the spacing between lines of text on a page and can be set as single, double or multiple lines. The default line spacing is *single.* Manuscripts and legal documents are usually typed in double line spacing in order for changes, annotations or corrections to be made. This is ***single line spacing*** This is ***single line spacing*** This is ***double line spacing*** This is ***double line spacing***

Tables	A table is a grid consisting of rows and columns to display text and numbers. Tables can be formatted to display borders and shading.		
	TITLE	**LEVEL**	**Start Date**
	Functional Skills ICT	Level 1	09/09/2010
	Functional Skills ICT	Level 2	10/09/2010

Columns	Handy for creating newsletters and leaflets, columns enable text to flow from the end of one column........	....to the top of the next column (like in a newspaper)

Formatted and edited information can be presented in a variety of different layouts. The layout of information should be appropriate, for example a poster may be presented differently to a business letter.

Different layout techniques that can be applied to information include the following:

Margins are the space between the edge of the paper and the text on the page. left, right, top and bottom page margins can be increased or decreased

Candidate Name

This text is in single line spacing and is left aligned.

This text is in double line spacing and is

justified.

This text is in single line spacing and is centred on the page

This text is in Time New Roman is right

Page 1 of 1

Headers and footers appear at the top and/or bottom of each of the pages in a document, and include dates, numbering, filenames and/or author name

Page numbering can be applied automatically to the top or bottom of a document, spreadsheet, report or slide. Page numbers will automatically display in sequential order for each page. Page numbers can be formatted to appear as Roman Numerals or letters, e.g. i, ii, iii or a, b, c etc

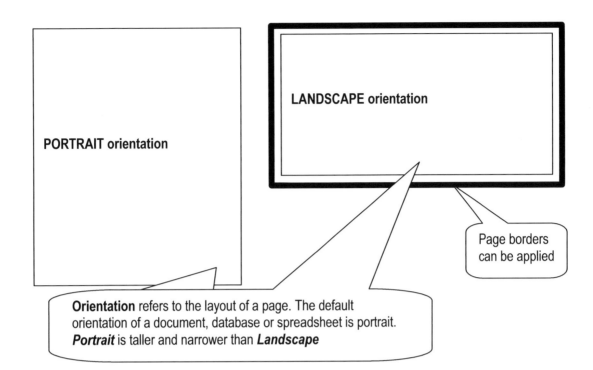

PORTRAIT orientation

LANDSCAPE orientation

Page borders can be applied

Orientation refers to the layout of a page. The default orientation of a document, database or spreadsheet is portrait. *Portrait* is taller and narrower than *Landscape*

Candidate Name

This is the first page in a 2 page document.
This is the first page in a 2 page document.
This is the first page in a 2 page document.
This is the first page in a 2 page document.
This is the first page in a 2 page document.
This is the first page in a 2 page document.

Page 1 of 2

Candidate Name

This is the second page in a 2 page document.
This is the second page in a 2 page document.
This is the second page in a 2 page document.
This is the second page in a 2 page document.
This is the second page in a 2 page document.
This is the second page in a 2 page document.

Page 2 of 2

Page breaks. A *soft* page break is automatically inserted when text reaches the end of a page and needs to continue on a separate page. A *hard* page break is inserted by the user wherever a new page is required.

Business Letter Layout

A business letter is a formal type of correspondence which is presented on letter headed paper (e.g. the letter contains the company's name and address and logo at the top, side or bottom of the letter).

A letter should be dated, include the recipient's name and address (a recipient is someone who receives) and also a subject line if appropriate. The body of the letter should be written in concise, business language.

A letter addressed to a person by name, such as **Dear Mr Smith**, should end with **Yours sincerely**. The first part, Dear Mr Smith, is called a *salutation* and the closing part of the letter is called a *complimentary close*). A letter addressed to Dear Sir or Madam should close with **Yours faithfully**.

At least 5 spaces should follow the complimentary close and the sender's name and position to allow for a signature.

If there is another document, cheque or other item enclosed with the letter this should be indicated by typing **Enc** or **Enc(s)** at least 2 spaces beneath the sender's name and position.

See the example below:

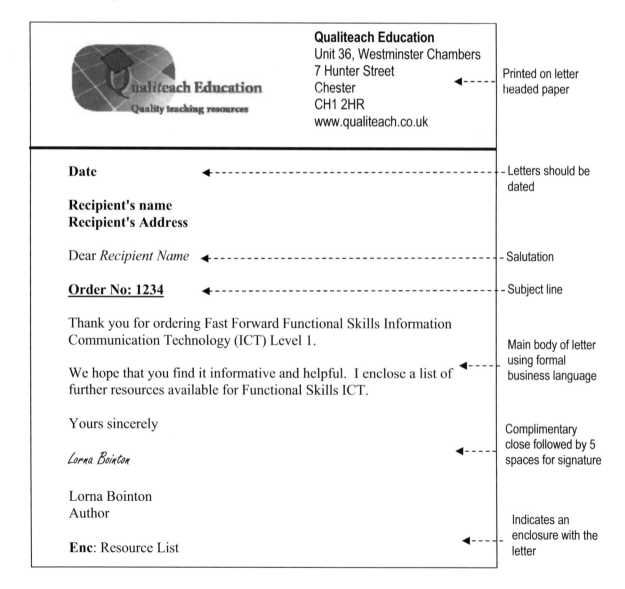

Help Sheets

7.1a

To find out how to do it, follow the instructions below

Editing Techniques

Insert text

- Click the cursor into position and start typing. Existing text will move along the line to accommodate the new text being entered. Press the Spacebar between each word.

Overtype

- Click the cursor into position and press the **Insert** key on the keyboard. Start typing and the newly inserted text will overtype the existing text.

Delete text

One character at a time

- Position the cursor in front of text and press the Delete key or position cursor at the end of text and use the Backspace key (the Delete key deletes text to the right of the current cursor position and Backspace deletes text to the left of the cursor position). Pressing the Delete or Backspace key once will delete a single character or space. Repeat to delete multiple characters/spaces.

Whole word

- Position the cursor in front of the word. Hold down the **CTRL** key on the keyboard and then press the Delete key. Position the cursor at the end of the word, hold down the **CTRL** key and press the Backspace key.

Cut, Copy and Paste

- Before text can be copied or moved it must first be selected. Position the cursor within a word and double click the left mouse button to select the whole word. Alternatively, position cursor in front of text and then, holding down the left mouse button, drag the mouse over the text to highlight (select) it.
- **To copy text**: select the **Copy** button From the **Home** tab and the **Clipboard** group
- **To cut text**: select the **Cut** button From the **Home** tab and the **Clipboard** group
- Position the cursor in the new location on the page and then click the **Paste** button (**Home** tab and **Clipboard** group)

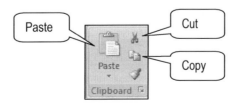

Drag and Drop

The drag and drop method enables text or objects to be copied or moved to another location within a document by using the mouse to drag the selected text/object and then releasing or 'dropping' it in the desired location.

- **To move text**: move the mouse arrow over selected text and then drag the text to the desired position. Release the mouse button.
- **To copy text**: repeat the above procedure but hold down the **Ctrl** key whilst dragging (the mouse arrow will display the copy symbol +)

Undo and Redo

- The Quick Access Toolbar displays the Undo and Redo buttons.
- Click the Undo button to undo an action. Click the Redo button to re-do an action

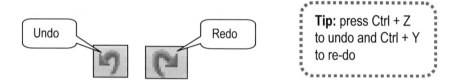

Undo   Redo

Tip: press Ctrl + Z to undo and Ctrl + Y to re-do

Replace text

- **Microsoft® Word, Excel, PowerPoint:** from the **Home** tab and the **Editing** group select the **Replace** command
- **Microsoft® Access:** from the **Home** tab and the **Find** group select the **Replace** command
- Type in the word or words to be found in the **Find What** box
- Type in the word or words which will replace the specified text in the **Replace With** box
- To replace each occurrence of a word individually select the **Replace** button or, to replace the word each time it occurs throughout a Microsoft® Word document, Excel spreadsheet, PowerPoint presentation or Access database click **Replace All**.

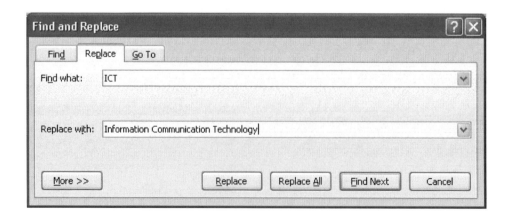

- A dialog box will appear showing the amount of replacements made. Click OK to confirm the replacements. Click **Close** to close the **Replace** dialog box.

Check Spelling

- **Microsoft® Word, Excel and PowerPoint**: From the **Review** tab and the **Proofing** group, select the **Spelling & Grammar** command (Word) or the **Spelling** command (Excel, PowerPoint).

- **Microsoft® Access**: From the **Home** tab and the **Proofing** group, select the **Spelling** command ![Spelling]

- The Spelling tool will display spelling errors and provide suggested replacements. Select a suggestion or click **Ignore** if you know that the word is correct (click **Ignore All** to ignore all instances of the word or **Change All** to change each instance of the word to the suggested spelling). A dialog box will appear at completion of the spelling check. Click OK to confirm.

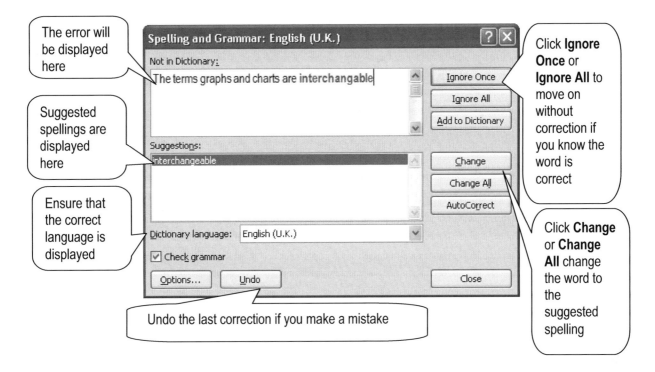

Formatting Techniques

Fonts, sizes, styles and colour

- Select the text to be formatted and then select a font type, font size, font style (bold, italics, underline) or font colour from the **Font** group (**Home** tab).

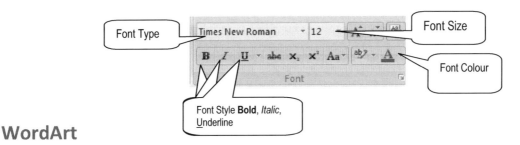

WordArt

- From the **Insert** tab, select **WordArt**. Click a WordArt style. Enter text into the dialog box and click OK. Select WordArt text to see the **WordArt Tools/Format** tab.

Bullets and Numbering

- Highlight the list and then select the **Bullets** or **Numbering** button from the **Home** tab and the **Paragraph** group.

Line Spacing

- Select the text or position the cursor within a paragraph and then select the **Line Spacing** button from the **Home** tab and the **Paragraph** group. Select an option from the drop down menu.

Alignment

- Select the text and then select one of the **Alignment** buttons from the **Home** tab and the **Paragraph** group (the alignment options are: left, centre, right, justify in Microsoft® Word and PowerPoint and Left, Centre and Right in Microsoft® Excel and Access).

Left, Centre, Right, Justify

Tabs

- Click the **Tab Style** button (left hand side of Ruler Bar as shown below) to select the desired tab style, e.g. left, right, centre, decimal (decimal tabs are used with prices etc to line up the decimal point).
- Click the Ruler Bar in the desired position to create a tab stop. The tabs are displayed on the Ruler Bar (see below).
- Press the **Tab** key to move the cursor to each tab stop position.

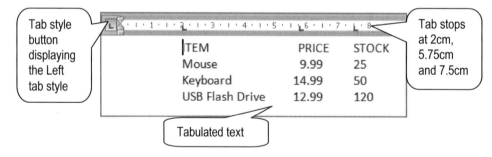

Tab style button displaying the Left tab style

Tab stops at 2cm, 5.75cm and 7.5cm

Tabulated text

ITEM	PRICE	STOCK
Mouse	9.99	25
Keyboard	14.99	50
USB Flash Drive	12.99	120

Tables

- From the **Insert** tab select **Table.**
- Select **Insert Table** from the drop down list.
- Choose the number of rows and columns that you need for the table and click **OK.**

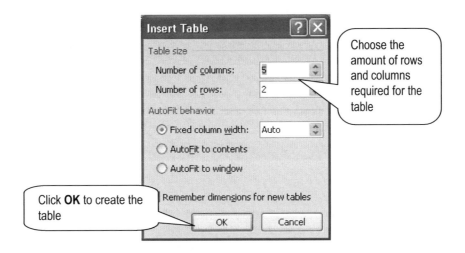

Choose the amount of rows and columns required for the table

Click **OK** to create the table

Borders and shading

- Select the table or the row(s) or column(s) to be formatted and then select the **Shading** button from the **Table Tools/Design** tab to apply or remove colour. Select the **Borders** button to apply or remove borders.

Select the shading button

Select a border style from the drop down list

Tip: Gridlines are different to borders and do not appear on printouts of a table.

Page Border

- For a page border, select the **Page Border** button from the **Page Layout** tab and **Page Background** group.

Layout Techniques

Margins

- **Microsoft® Word, Excel**: select the **Margins** button from the **Page Layout** tab and the **Page Setup** group. Choose a margin setting or select **Custom Margins** to choose your own margin sizes.
- The **Page Setup** dialog box will appear. Select the top, bottom, left and right margins and click **OK**

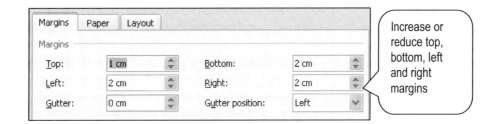

Increase or reduce top, bottom, left and right margins

- **Microsoft® Access**: select the **Office Button**, **Print** and then **Print Preview.** Select the **Margins** button. Choose a margin setting from the drop down list. To choose different margin settings, click the **Page Layout** dialog box launcher icon. From the **Print Options** tab, select margins as required and click OK.

Orientation

- **Microsoft® Word, Excel**: from the **Page Layout** tab, select **Orientation**. Choose Portrait or Landscape

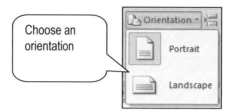

Choose an orientation

- **Microsoft® PowerPoint:** From the **Design** tab, select the **Slide Orientation** button and choose an orientation from the drop down list.
- **Microsoft® Access:** select the **Office Button**, **Print** and then **Print Preview**. Select either **Portrait** or **Landscape** buttons from the **Page Layout** group

Headers and Footers

- **Microsoft® Word:** From the **Insert** tab, select **Header** or **Footer**

Choose Header or Footer

- Select the type of header or footer that you want from the menu or select **Edit Header/Footer** to make changes to an existing header or footer. The **Header & Footer Tools** ribbon becomes available.
- Enter the required information in the header or footer area
- Select the **Close Header and Footer** button

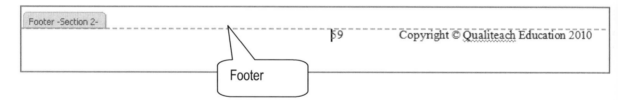

Footer -Section 2-

59   Copyright © Qualiteach Education 2010

Footer

- **Microsoft® Excel:** From the **Insert** tab, select **Header & Footer.**
- The **Header & Footer Tools** ribbon becomes available. Enter the required information in the header or footer area or select a field, such as Date & Time, to insert. To insert an automatic filename, author name or other fields, select the **Quick Parts** button and then select **Field.** Choose a category, such as Document Information, and a field name, such as Filename. Click OK to insert the field.

- **Microsoft® PowerPoint:** From the **Insert** tab, select **Header & Footer.**
- The **Header and Footer** dialog box appears. Enter text that is to appear in the footer in the **Footer** box, select **Date & Time** to include a date on the slides, select **Slide Number** to insert a number on each slide. Click **Apply to All** to apply the footer to all slides or Apply to add the footer to the currently selected slide.

Columns

- Select the **Columns** command from the **Page Layout** tab. Choose the desired amount of columns. Select **More Columns** to see further options, such as column width and spacing.

Page Numbers

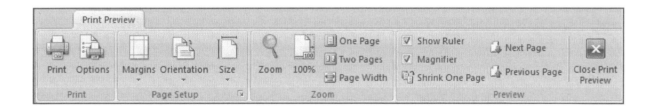

- From the **Insert** tab and the **Header & Footer** group, select the **Page Number** button
- Select an option from the drop down list, e.g. Top of Page or Bottom of Page, and select an alignment from the submenu. The **Header & Footer Tools** ribbon becomes available.
- Select the **Close Header and Footer** button

Page Breaks

- To create a manual (hard) page break, position the cursor where the page break is to be inserted and then press the **Ctrl** key and the Enter key.
- Alternatively, select the **Page Layout** tab and then select the **Breaks** command. Select **Page** from the drop down list.
- Page breaks can be viewed on the page by selecting the **Show/Hide** button from the **Home** tab.

·················Page Break·················

- To delete a page break (only possible with a manually inserted page break and not a soft page break) click onto the page break and press **Delete**

Print Preview

- To check your document for layout and correct page structure, select the **Office Button** and then select the **Print** arrow. From the sub-menu, select **Print Preview**.

- Choose commands from the ribbon:

- Exit Print Preview by selecting the **Close Print Preview** button.

Vertical Text Alignment

- From the **Page Layout** tab, select the **Page Setup** dialog box launcher icon. Select the **Layout** tab. From the **Vertical Alignment** drop down box, select the desired vertical alignment (default vertical alignment is **Top**). Click OK.

Match Makers

Match the correct answers with the questions below:

1.	The distance between the edge of the paper and the text?	a.	Portrait
2.	The default orientation of a Microsoft Office document?	b.	Margin
3.	**Arial** is an example of?	c.	A page break
4.	Pressing Control and Enter creates?	d.	A font type

Enter your answers below:

1.		2.		3.		4.	

As Easy As....

1. The default alignment in a Microsoft® Word document is?

A	Right	☐
B	Justified	☐
C	Left	☐
D	Centre	☐

2. Inserting and deleting words in a document is an example of which type of technique?

A	Editing	☐
B	Formatting	☐
C	Layout	☐
D	Checking	☐

Practice Makes Perfect

Practical Exercise 1

1. Create a new document in Microsoft® Word and save it as **Format.docx.**

2. Change the orientation to landscape.

3. Change the left and right margins to 2cm.

4. Add a page number to the footer and your name to the header.

5. Create a page break so that the document has two pages. Re-save the document.

Practical Exercise 2

1. Enter the following text (with deliberate spelling errors) on the first page of the document:

> LAYOUT
>
> Thiss informationn iss presented in ssingle linne spacing and is left aligned. The margins are set as 2cm on the left and right and the orientation is landscape. A header has been added at the top and a foooter has been adddded at the bottom of the doccument.

2. Check the spelling of the text that you have just entered and correct the errors. Edit the text by doing the following:

    *   Delete the word 'presented' and enter the word 'formatted'
    *   Add the word 'document' in front of the word 'margins'
    *   Replace the word 'added' with 'inserted' wherever it occurs (twice)

3. Resave the document.

Practical Exercise 3

1. Format the heading LAYOUT to be in a different font type (your choice), a larger font size, a dark blue font colour, bold and centred.

2. Format the rest of the text to be Arial, 12, justified and in double line spacing.

3. On page 2 enter the heading ORIENTATION and create a bulleted list below this heading with the following information:

    *   Portrait
    *   Landscape

4. Save and close the document.

Graphics

Graphics are Images or pictures which can be inserted from the Clipart gallery, from a Clipart image DVD or from a stored location on your computer (such as digital photographs).

Graphics can be resized and cropped to make them suitable for inclusion in documents. Image size can be increased or decreased and parts of an image can be removed by using the cropping tool. Images can be positioned accurately on a page by using the Picture tools.

The resolution of an image refers to the amount of pixels (picture elements) or tiny squares that make up the picture. More pixels mean better quality but also higher file sizes. Resolution of a printed image needs to be higher than an image which will be viewed on-screen, such as on a web page.

When an image is selected it is surrounded by small blobs – these are resizing handles. When the mouse arrow is placed over a resizing handle, the mouse pointer turns into a double headed black arrow. Drag the mouse inwards and/or downwards to reduce the size or drag outwards and upwards to increase the size. To ensure that images maintain the original proportions without distortion, the Lock Aspect Ratio option should be selected before resizing the height OR the width. Always resize manually via a corner resizing handle.

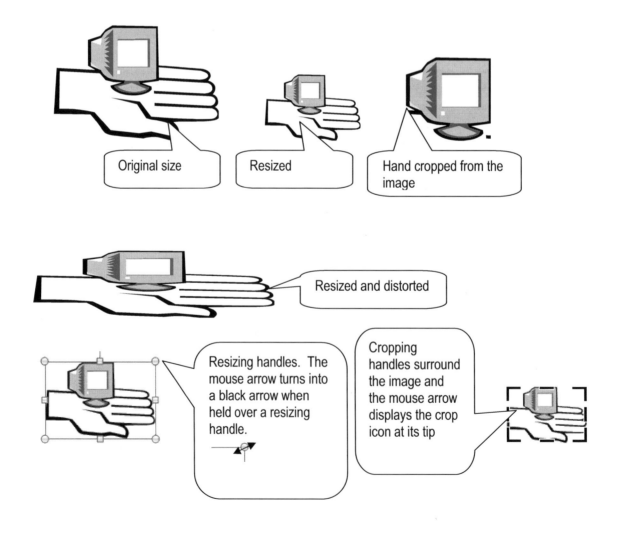

Original size

Resized

Hand cropped from the image

Resized and distorted

Resizing handles. The mouse arrow turns into a black arrow when held over a resizing handle.

Cropping handles surround the image and the mouse arrow displays the crop icon at its tip

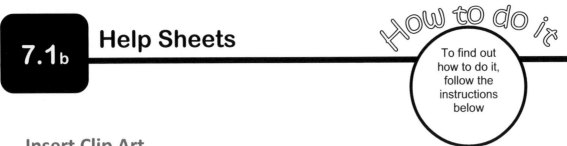

Insert Clip Art

- Position the cursor where the image is to be inserted. Select the **Insert** tab.
- Select the **Clip Art** button and the Clip Art task pane will open.
- Type an image name/description into the **Search for** box (e.g. computer) and press the **Go** button.
- The Clip Art gallery will display images matching the search words that you entered. Select an image to insert it into the document or slide.

Insert an image from file

- Position the cursor in the document or slide where the image is to be inserted. Select the **Insert** tab.
- Select the **Picture** button and the **Insert Picture** dialog box will appear.
- Find and select the required image file and then click **Insert.**

Resize an image

- Click the image and resizing handles will appear around the image.
- Move the mouse pointer over a corner resizing handle (always drag from a corner handle to maintain image proportions) and drag inwards and downwards to reduce the size or outwards and upwards to increase the size.
- Images can also be resized accurately by selecting **Shape Height** or **Shape Width** measurements from the **Picture Tools/Layout** tab and the **Size** group. Choose whether to change the height or width measurement.

Crop an image

- Select the image and then select the **Crop** tool from the **Picture Tools/Image** tab.
- Move the mouse pointer over one of the crop handles and drag to crop parts of the image.

Wrap an image

- Click on the image and then select the **Text Wrapping** command from the **Picture Tools/Image** tab.
- Select a wrapping style from the drop down list:

  In Line with Text – this is the default wrapping style for inserted images. The image will be positioned on the same line as text.
  Square – wraps text squarely around the image
  Tight – wraps text tightly around the image
  Behind Text – image will be positioned behind text
  In Front of Text – image will be positioned in front of text enabling free movement of the image on the page

Align an image

The **In Line With Text** wrapping style should be applied to a selected image before being aligned using the Alignment tools.

- Select the image. From the **Home** tab and the **Paragraph** group, select an Alignment button.

Position an image

If the **In Line With Text** wrapping style is applied, the Position commands will not work so choose a different wrapping style.

- Select the image and then select the **Picture Tools/Image** tab.
- Select the **Position** button.
- Select **More Layout Options** from the menu.
- Select the **Picture Position** tab and make changes to the current **Horizontal** and/or **Vertical** position of the image.
- Click **OK.**

Move an Image

- Position mouse pointer over image, hold down mouse button (black cross icon appears) and drag (will not work if In Line with Text wrapping style applied).

Reduce Image Resolution

- Select the image and then select the **Picture Tools/Image** tab.
- Select the **Compress Pictures** command from the **Adjust** group. Tick the **Apply to selected pictures only** checkbox. Select the **Options** button and choose options (subject to how the image will be viewed), such as **Screen (150 ppi) good for web pages and projectors**. Click **OK.**

Activities

Match Makers

Match the correct answers with the questions below:

1.	Reducing image resolution reduces the amount of what in a picture?	a.	Position
2.	Behind Text is an example of which Picture tool?	b.	Pixels
3.	Images inserted from a stored gallery or DVD are called?	c.	Wrapping
4.	Images can be placed accurately on a page by using which tool?	d.	Clipart

Enter your answers below:

1.		2.		3.		4.	

As Easy As....

1. To maintain original proportions of a graphic, it should be resized manually by which handle?

A	Corner handle	☐
B	Middle handle	☐
C	Crop handle	☐
D	Any of the selection handles	☐

2. Cropping does what to a picture?

A	Resizes the picture	☐
B	Chops bits off a picture	☐
C	Deletes the picture	☐
D	Affects image resolution	☐

Practical Exercise 1

1.   Create a new document in Microsoft® Word and save it as **Graphic.docx.**

2.   Enter the heading **FUNCTIONAL SKILLS ICT.** Format with a large font size and centre across the page.

3.   Type the following text beneath the heading:

The image is cropped and resized. To ensure that the text wraps to the left of the image, the **Tight** wrapping style will be applied and the image moved to the right of the text.

4.   Format the text to be Arial, 12, justified and in double line spacing.

5.   Insert the following Clipart graphic of a computer beneath the text.

Practical Exercise 2

1.   Crop the image so that only the monitor remains.

2.   Resize the image so that it is 6cm in height.

Practical Exercise 3

1.   Apply the **Tight** wrapping style to the image.

2.   Move the image so that it is positioned to the right of the text and the text wraps to the left of the image.

3.   Save and close the document.

Drawing Tools

Drawing tools are used to create shapes, such as circles, ovals, squares, text boxes, arrows etc.

See the examples below:

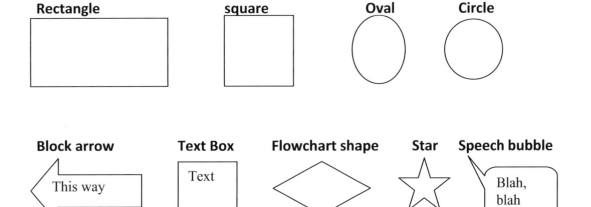

Rectangle

square

Oval

Circle

Block arrow

This way

Text Box

Text

Flowchart shape

Star

Speech bubble

Blah, blah

Shapes can be formatted with colour, lines and text and can be structured to appear in a different order (i.e. Bring to front, Send to back etc) and then grouped together to make one object. In the example below there are 3 shapes, formatted with different colours and line styles:

The shapes can be displayed in a different order:

The diamond shape is brought forward in front of the star shape

The diamond shape is sent backwards, behind the circle

How to do it

To find out how to do it, follow the instructions below

The following instructions work with Microsoft® Word, PowerPoint and Excel.

Create Shapes

- Select the **Insert** tab and then, from the **Illustrations** group, select the **Shapes** command.

- Choose a shape from the drop-down menu.

- Position the mouse pointer on the page where the shape is to be inserted.

- The mouse pointer displays as a black crosshair icon

- Either click the mouse to insert the shape or drag the shape to the required size

> **Tip**: Hold down the **Shift** key when creating a rectangle or oval shape to create a perfect square or circle

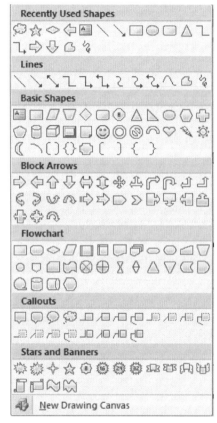

Insert Text

- Right click the shape and select **Add Text**. The cursor will be positioned within the shape. Enter the desired text. Format the text as required.

Format a shape

- Select the shape and then, from the **Drawing Tools/Format** tab (may be displayed as the **Text Box Tools** depending on type of shape inserted) and the **Shape Styles** group, select the **Shape Fill** button. Choose a colour or select a different formatting option from the drop-down menu (gradient, texture, picture, pattern, no fill or more fill colours)

- To format a shape border, select the shape and then, from the **Drawing Tools/Format** tab and the **Shape Styles** group, select the **Shape Outline** button. Select an option from the menu (such as Outline colour, weight or dash style)

Select Shapes

- Click an individual shape to select it.
- Hold down the **CTRL** key and click each shape to select multiple shapes

Order Shapes

- Select a shape and then, from the **Drawing Tools/Format** tab (may be displayed as the **Text Box Tools** depending on type of shape inserted) and the **Arrange** group, select the **Bring to Front** or **Send to Back** buttons and choose an option from the drop-down menu.

Group shapes

- Select each of the shapes and then right click and select **Grouping** and then **Group**

Ungrouped Images   **Grouped images**

Drawing Tools Ribbon:

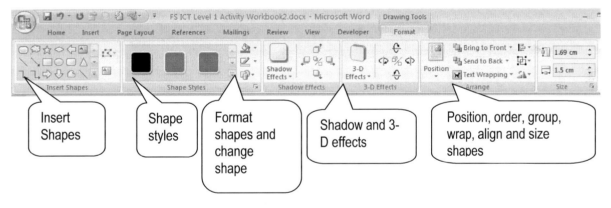

Match Makers

Match the correct answers with the questions below:

1.	Use this command to bring a shape in front of another?	a.	Group
2.	Use this command to join shapes together as one object?	b.	Ordering
3.	To select multiple shapes you need to hold down this key?	c.	Flowchart
4.	Shapes can be used to create which type of diagram showing sequential steps in a task or project?	d.	Ctrl

Enter your answers below:

1.		2.		3.		4.	

As Easy As....

1. Which key should be pressed whilst creating a rectangle shape to create a perfect square?

A	Ctrl	☐
B	Shift	☐
C	Tab	☐
D	ALT	☐

2. Which of the following actions would allow a user to enter text into a shape?

A	Left click and then select **Add Text**	☐
B	Right click and then select **Insert Text**	☐
C	Left click and select **Enter Text**	☐
D	Right click and select **Add Text**	☐

Practical Exercise 1

1. Create a new document in Microsoft® Word and save it as **Shape.docx**

2. Insert a square shape, a circle and a triangle

3. Format the square with a red fill colour

4. Format the circle with a green fill colour

5. Format the triangle with a yellow fill colour

Practical Exercise 2

1. Position the triangle on top of the square

2. Position the circle on top of the triangle:

3. Re-order the shapes so that the triangle is in front of the circle (tip: bring forward):

4. Add the following text to the triangle: **IN FRONT** and format with appropriate font size.

5. Group the three shapes together as one object.

6. Resave and close the document

Presentations

A presentation is a set of slides which are presented in a specific order to an audience or as a continuously looping presentation in a reception area. A presentation which is presented to an audience is called a slide show. A presentation can use automatic timings or be controlled by a presenter with mouse clicks.

A presentation can include text, bulleted lists, images, charts, video and audio files.

To ensure consistency throughout a presentation, the formatting, such as fonts, font sizes, font colours, font styles, background colour and logos and any other standard content (i.e. any content which will appear on every slide in the presentation) is applied to a master slide which is a type of template on which slides within the presentation are based.

Slide content can be added to a slide using either Outline or Normal view, but images will only display in Normal View.

A slide show can be run using the Slide Show view.

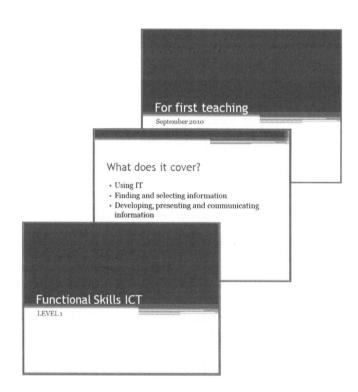

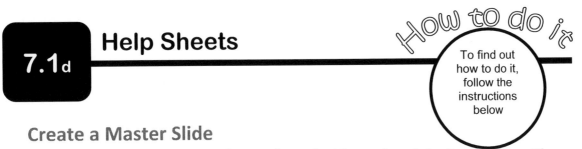
Create a Master Slide

- Select the **Slide Master** button from the **View** tab and the **Presentation Views** group
- Format the slide areas as desired (select formatting tools from the **Home** tab)

Apply Background Colour

- Ensure that Master Slide view is selected. Select the **Background Styles** button. Select **Format Background**. Select the **Color** button and choose a colour. Click **Apply to All**. Click **Close**.

Normal View

- Select the **Normal** button from the **View** tab.

Slide Show View

- Select the **Slide Show** button from the **View** tab.

Insert New Slide

- Ensure that Normal view is selected and then select the **New Slide** button from the **Home** tab. Select a slide layout.

Change Slide Layout

- In Normal view, select the **Layout** button from the **Home** tab. Select a slide layout.

Insert a new slide

Change the slide layout

Diagrams and Flowcharts

- In Normal view, select the **Smart Art** button from the **Insert** tab. Select a diagram or flowchart shape and click **OK**.

Select to insert diagrams or flowcharts

Choose a type of diagram

Print

- From the **Office Button** select **Print** and then select **Print** from the sub-menu.
- To print each slide, select the **All** option button in the **Print** section. Ensure that **Slides** is selected in the **Print What** section. Click **OK**.

Print handouts

- From the **Print What** box, select **Handouts**. Select the amount of slides to appear on each page from the **Slides per page** menu. Click **OK**.

Handouts 3 per page

Handouts 6 per page

Insert Objects (graphs/tables)

- From the **Home** tab, select the **Title and Content** slide layout
- To insert a chart, click the **Insert Chart** icon. Choose a chart type and click **OK**. Enter data into the spreadsheet to create the chart and then close the spreadsheet on completion. The **Chart Tools** tab becomes available when the chart is selected.
- To insert a table, select the **Insert Table** icon. Choose the required amount of table rows/columns and click **OK**. The **Table Tools** tab becomes active when the table is selected.

Select an icon, such as Table or Chart

Movies, SmartArt and images can also be inserted

7.1d **Activities**

Try the activities below to test yourself on the previous section

Match Makers

Match the correct answers with the questions below:

1.	This ensures consistency of formatting in throughout a presentation?	a. Title and Content
2.	A printout showing 3 slides on one page is called a?	b. Master Slide
3.	A presentation consisting of slides delivered in a specific sequence and usually accompanying a talk?	c. Handout
4.	Tables can be inserted using which slide layout?	d. Slide Show

Enter your answers below:

1.		2.		3.		4.	

As Easy As....

1. A slide show with automatic timings is suited to which type of presentation?

A	A presentation for a sales pitch	☐
B	A continuous looping slide show in a reception area	☐
C	A slide show to accompany a talk by a presenter	☐
D	A slide show presented by an interviewee in a job interview	☐

2. Content can be inserted onto a slide in Outline view and which other view?

A	Slide Show	☐
B	Normal	☐
C	Slide Sorter	☐
D	Print Preview	☐

© Lorna Bointon, Qualiteach Education 2010

Practice Makes Perfect

Practical Exercise 1

1. Create a new presentation in Microsoft® PowerPoint and save it as **Functional.pptx.**

2. Using the master slide, format the background with a colour of your choice. Format the heading, subheading and bullet text with fonts, sizes and colour of your choice.

3. Create a Title Slide with the heading **FUNCTIONAL SKILLS ICT** and the subheading **LEVEL 1.**

4. Insert a new slide to hold a title and bulleted text. Enter the heading: **What does it cover?** Enter the following bulleted text:

   - Using IT
   - Finding and selecting information
   - Developing, presenting and communicating information

5. Insert a new slide to contain a heading and subheading. Enter the following heading: **For First Teaching** and enter the subheading **September 2010.** Re-save the presentation.

Practical Exercise 2

1. Create a new slide with the heading **Software Applications**. Insert a table with the following text:

Word Processing	Letters, posters, leaflets, information sheets, memos, reports
Spreadsheets	Accounts, budgets, charts
Presentations	Slide shows, display of digital content
Databases	Customer names and addresses, stock details

2. Insert a new slide with a Title only slide layout and enter the heading **Information Communication Technology.** Insert a Clipart picture of a computer.

3. Resave the presentation and close.

Section 8 ▶

Developing, Presenting and Communicating Information

Data

Use appropriate software to meet requirements of straightforward data-handling task

Numerical Data

A spreadsheet is used for performing calculations and is displayed as a grid containing rows and columns. The rows are horizontal and the columns are vertical.

A row is numbered and a column is lettered (e.g. column A and row 1). There are many rows and columns in a spreadsheet. Both rows and columns can be deleted if required or extra rows/columns inserted. The intersection between a row and a column is called a cell. The name of the cell is made up of the column letter and the row number (e.g. cell A1) and is referred to as a cell reference. Calculations in a spreadsheet are created using cell references rather than the numerical data. For example:

=A1+B1   instead of   =2+10

This ensures that, when the numbers change, the formula re-calculates.

Every formula starts with the equals sign = and uses arithmetic operators for addition, subtraction, division and multiplication:

+   Addition

-       Subtraction

/   Division

*   Multiplication

	A	B	C	D
1	Item	Amount	Cost	Total
2	Mouse	2	9.99	=B2*C2
3	Keyboard	1	14.99	=B3*C3
4	Memory stick	3	12.99	=B4*C4

The total cost of purchases uses the multiplication operator to multiply the cost by the amount (note how cell references are used

Multiple cells are referred to as a cell range. The cell range, when used in a formula uses the first and last cell in the range separated by a colon : (e.g. A1:C10). Cell ranges are used in formulas and functions in the following way:

=SUM(B3:B7)   this formula uses the SUM function to find the total of the cell range B3 to B7

	A	B
1	Ryan's 18th Birthday Party	
2		
3	Venue	£150.00
4	Catering	£350.00
5	Entertainment	£250.00
6	Postal costs	£10.00
7		
8	Total Costs	£760.00

Other functions include average, count, maximum and minimum. Numbers in a spreadsheet can be formatted to display a specified amount of decimal places or no decimal places (whole numbers called *integers*). Numbers can also be formatted as percentages or currency.

The **Fill Handle** is located in the bottom right corner of a selected cell. When the mouse pointer is positioned over the fill handle, the mouse pointer turns into a black cross. Hold down the mouse button and drag to copy the formula into adjacent cells ✚

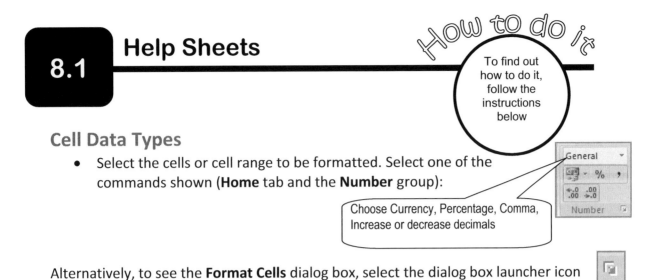

Cell Data Types

- Select the cells or cell range to be formatted. Select one of the commands shown (**Home** tab and the **Number** group):

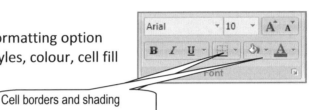

Choose Currency, Percentage, Comma, Increase or decrease decimals

Alternatively, to see the **Format Cells** dialog box, select the dialog box launcher icon

Cell Formatting

- Select the cells and then choose a formatting option from the **Font** group (fonts, sizes, styles, colour, cell fill colour, cell borders).

Cell borders and shading

Centre Across Columns

- Select the amount of columns that the title will span and then click the **Merge & Center** button (**Home** tab, **Alignment** group).

Wrap Text

- Select the cell and then click the **Wrap Text** button (**Home** tab, **Alignment** group).

Create a Formula

- Enter the **Equals** sign (=) followed by the first cell reference. Enter the arithmetic operator, such as +, -, /, * followed by the second cell reference (e.g. =A1*B1).

Use the Sum Function

- Click into the cell in which the result will be displayed. Select the **SUM** button (**Home** tab and **Editing** group). The SUM formula (e.g. =SUM(A1:C10) will display on the spreadsheet; click the **SUM** button again to complete the function.

- You can also enter a SUM function manually: type the equals sign (=), followed by the function name SUM. Type an open round bracket and then type the cell range separated by a colon (:). Close the bracket, e.g. =SUM(A1:C10).

Page Layout

- Commands such as Margins, Orientation (Portrait/Landscape) can be selected from the **Page Layout** tab and the **Page Setup** group. For other page layout options, such as headers and footers and to display gridlines and/or row and column headings, click the dialog box launcher icon to open the **Page Setup** dialog box.

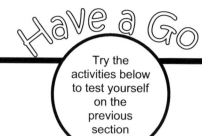

Match Makers

Match the correct answers with the questions below:

1.	Formulas always start with this?	a	/
2.	This arithmetic operator is used for division	b	:
3.	This arithmetic operator is used for multiplication	c	=
4.	This separates a cell range?	d	*

Enter your answers below:

1.		2.		3.		4.	

As Easy As....

1.   The handle used to replicate the contents of a cell over other cells is called?

A	A cell handle	☐
B	A replicate handle	☐
C	A copy handle	☐
D	A fill handle	☐

2.   The SUM command is an example of a?

A	Function	☐
B	Formatting tool	☐
C	Logical operator	☐
D	Arithmetic operator	☐

Practical Exercise 1

1.   Create a new spreadsheet in Microsoft® Excel and save it as **party.xlsx.**

2.   Enter the data into the spreadsheet as shown below:

	A	B
1	Ryan's 18th Birthday Party	
2		
3	Venue	£150.00
4	Catering	£350.00
5	Entertainment	£250.00
6	Postal costs	£10.00

3.   Format the title as bold and centred across columns A and B. Format the spreadsheet data with fonts, font sizes, font styles and alignment of your own choice.

4.   Click into cell A8 and enter the text: **Total Costs.**

5.   Using the SUM function, find the total of the cell range B3:B6.

6.   Format the cell range B3:B8 with the currency symbol and 2 decimal places:

	A	B
1	Ryan's 18th Birthday Party	
2		
3	Venue	£150.00
4	Catering	£350.00
5	Entertainment	£250.00
6	Postal costs	£10.00
7		
8	Total Costs	£760.00

7.   Re-save the spreadsheet and close.

Graphs and Charts

A chart enables a user to see the results of spreadsheet data in a graphical format.

For example, the following data is easier to see as a pie chart:

	A	B
1	Ryan's 18th Birthday Party	
2		
3	Venue	£150.00
4	Catering	£350.00
5	Entertainment	£250.00
6	Postal costs	£10.00
7		
8	Total Costs	£760.00

Spreadsheet data

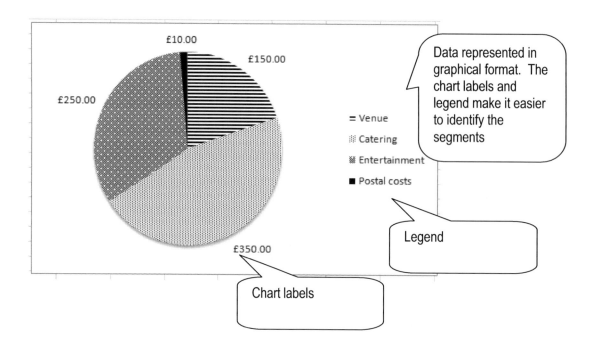

Data represented in graphical format. The chart labels and legend make it easier to identify the segments

Legend

Chart labels

A pie chart is a suitable format for a chart with one data series, e.g. one row or one column of data.

A legend is the key to the data in the chart – in the chart above the legend identifies which segments represent each piece of data (venue, catering, entertainment, postal costs). The chart labels display the cost of each item.

Different types of data require different chart types. See some sample charts below:

Bar/Column Chart:

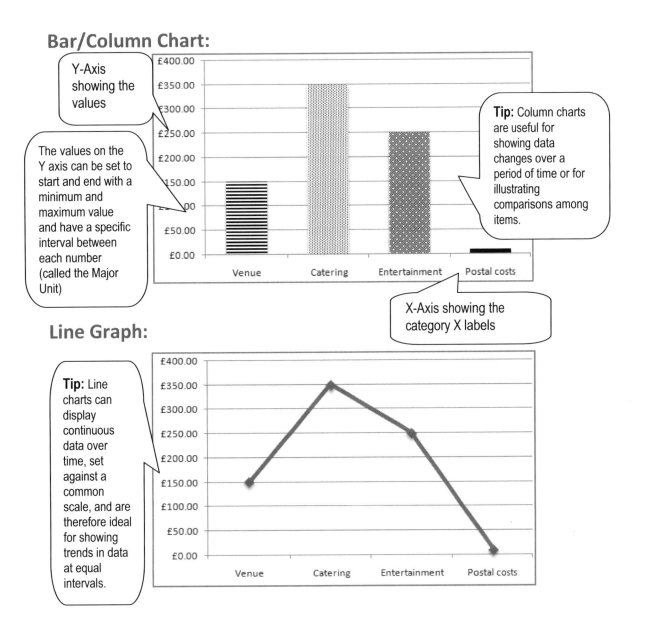

Y-Axis showing the values

The values on the Y axis can be set to start and end with a minimum and maximum value and have a specific interval between each number (called the Major Unit)

Tip: Column charts are useful for showing data changes over a period of time or for illustrating comparisons among items.

X-Axis showing the category X labels

Line Graph:

Tip: Line charts can display continuous data over time, set against a common scale, and are therefore ideal for showing trends in data at equal intervals.

Comparison chart (showing first choices and second choices)

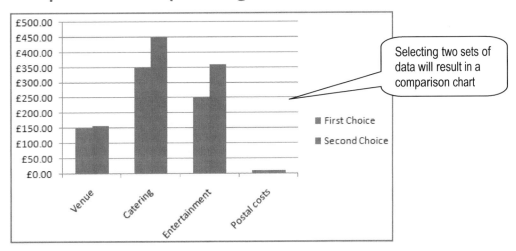

Selecting two sets of data will result in a comparison chart

■ First Choice
■ Second Choice

To find out how to do it, follow the instructions below

Create a chart

- Select the data to be used in the chart.
- Select the **Insert** tab and then, from the **Charts** group, select a chart type command (pie, bar, line etc.).

Select a chart

- From the drop-down menu of the selected chart, select a sub-type.

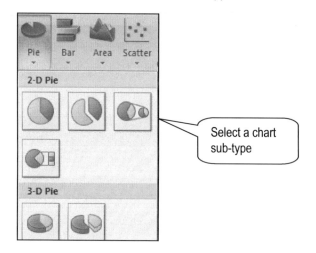

Select a chart sub-type

Apply titles

- Select the chart. From the **Chart Tools/Layout** tab and the **Labels** group, select the commands you need, such as chart title, axis titles, legend and/or data labels.

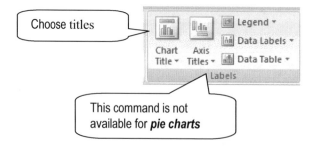

Choose titles

This command is not available for *pie charts*

- Choose the alignment of the title(s) and enter the required text.

Tip: Select **Chart Tools/Design** to change the style or type of chart and choose **Chart Tools/Format** to format the chart with different colours, gradients or textures.

Have a Go

Try the activities below to test yourself on the previous section

Match Makers

Match the correct answers with the questions below:

1.	A graph to show trends in data over a period of time?	a.	Comparison
2.	A graph showing the results of two sets of data?	b.	Column
3.	A graph showing data as segments?	c.	Line
4.	A graph that shows data changes over a period of time as vertical bars	d.	Pie

Enter your answers below:

1.		2.		3.		4.	

As Easy As....

1. Which of the following is the correct definition of a legend?

A	A key that identifies the different segments, columns or lines in a chart	☐
B	A key that displays values from the Y-axis	☐
C	A legend is a label which describes the x-axis	☐
D	A legend is the chart title	☐

2. Which of the following is a correct definition of a major unit?

A	The gap between each column in a chart	☐
B	A specific interval between each number on the value axis of a chart	☐
C	The minimum number on the value axis	☐
D	The maximum number on the value axis	☐

Practical Exercise 1

1. Open the **Party.xlsx** spreadsheet in Microsoft® Excel.

2. Create a pie chart from the cell range A3:B6.

3. Add **Value** data labels to the chart.

4. Retain the legend.

5. Add the title **Ryan's Party Pie**.

6. Format the segments with different fill colours.

7. Save the spreadsheet.

Practical Exercise 2

1. Create a column chart from the cell range A3:B6 beneath the pie chart.

2. Delete the legend.

3. Add the title **Ryan's Party Column**.

4. Add the title **Party Hire** to the horizontal X Axis.

5. Add the title **Party Costs** to the vertical Y Axis.

6. Save the spreadsheet and close.

Databases

A database stores data in a collection of related tables (e.g. Table 1: customer names and addresses, Table 2: account details and Table 3: stock details).

A table is made up of a list of related records (e.g. customer details, such as name and address). A record is made up of related fields (e.g. title, first name, last name, address 1, town, post code). A field is an item of information (e.g. John) beneath a field heading (e.g. First Name). It is important that the field headings are separated logically in order to query the data (for example, to find all customers with the surname Smith).

Example:

Field headings

Fields

Title	First Name	Last Name	Address 1	Town	City	Post Code
Mr	John	Smith	1 The House	Townsville	Bigham	BG1 1TH

A collection of related fields makes a record

Field names

It is important that the field headings are separated logically in order to query the data (for example, to find all customers with the surname Smith or to find customers from a specific city). A field name can be up to 64 characters long, including spaces. Microsoft® Office Access disallows the same field name within a table (duplicates). Field sizes and formats can be applied to fields. For example, a date may be formatted as a short date (01/01/2010) or a text field may be limited to 15 characters.

Data types

In order to organise data correctly, fields need to have data types applied according to the type of data that will be entered into the field. For example, dates should be formatted with the data type **Date/Time.** Other field data types include *Text* which is the default data type for text and alphanumeric data (e.g. data containing both text and numbers and also telephone numbers which include spaces), *Number* for numerical data with or without decimal places and *Currency* (£) for numerical data relating to costs. Data types can be selected for a field item from the Data Type drop-down list in Design View. If an incorrect data type is applied to a field in the design stage, the data may not sort properly at a later date (e.g. numerical data with a Text data type will not sort in numerical order).

Database Objects

A **table** is a collection of records.

Queries are used to look up specific data in a table.

Forms are used for data entry.

Reports are used to print out information from a database.

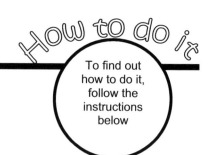
Table Design

- Create a new database by selecting **Start** and then **All Programs**. Select the **Microsoft® Office** folder and then **Microsoft® Office Access 2007**.

- The **Getting Started** window will open.

- Under the heading **New Blank Database,** select **Blank Database.**

- The **Blank Database** section appears in the **Getting Started** window. A filename is supplied by Microsoft® Access but this can be changed if desired by entering a file name into the **File Name** box. Ensure that the database saves in the correct drive/folder (the save location will be displayed under the filename).

- Click the yellow folder icon (**Browse**) to choose another location in which to save the database file. Ensure that the correct drive and/or folder is selected from the Look in box. Select OK.

- Select the **Create** button. To design the table with different field names and data types, select the **View** button and choose **Design View**.

- The **Save Table** message appears. Enter a name for the table and click OK.

- The table design opens enabling the design and creation of a table within the database.

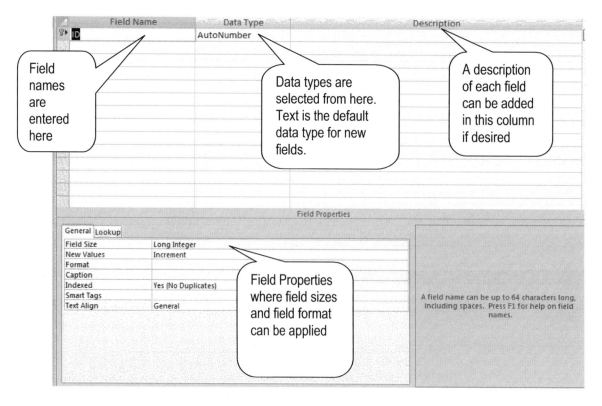

Field names are entered here

Data types are selected from here. Text is the default data type for new fields.

A description of each field can be added in this column if desired

Field Properties where field sizes and field format can be applied

- Close a database by selecting **Close Database** from the **Office Button.**

Have a Go

Try the activities below to test yourself on the previous section

Match Makers

Match the correct answers with the questions below:

1.	A collection of related data items?		a.	Field
2.	Data stored as a collection of related tables?		b.	Table
3.	A single data item?		c.	Record
4.	A collection of related records?		d.	Database

Enter your answers below:

1.		2.		3.		4.	

As Easy As....

1. Which of the following statements about field names is correct?

A	A field name can be more than 64 characters long	☐
B	Duplicate field names are allowed	☐
C	Field names should be separated logically	☐
D	All field names must have the same data type	☐

2. Which of the following is a correct definition of a data type?

A	If an incorrect data type is applied, the data may not sort properly	☐
B	Text data types should be applied to text only	☐
C	The Number data type should be applied to alphanumeric data	☐
D	Currency is the default data type	☐

Practical Exercise 1

1.   Create a new database called **Friends.accdb** in Microsoft® Access.

2.   Create a new table within the Friends database called **Birthdays** with the following design (keep the ID field as this will provide a unique reference for each record):

Field Heading	Data Type	Field Size/Format
First Name	Text	15
Last Name	Text	25
Date of Birth	Date/Time	Short Date

3.   Save and close the table and the **Friends** database.

Practical Exercise 2

1.   Create a new database called **Sales.accdb** in Microsoft® Access.

2.   Create a new table within the Sales database called **Stock** with the following design (keep the ID field as this will provide a unique reference for each record):

Field Heading	Data Type	Field Size/Format
Stock Item	Text	40
Amount in Stock	Number	Integer
Price	Currency	Currency

3.   Save and close the table and the **Sales** database.

Enter, Search, Sort, Edit Data

Did You Know?

Data must be entered correctly in order to sort correctly

Enter and edit data

The term 'data' is an item of information which can be entered into a document, spreadsheet or a database, such as a customer's name or address, an item's purchase price or a date. Data needs to be regularly updated to reflect current prices or changes in customer details, such as change of address. Data can be edited by amending existing data, deleting data and inserting new data.

Sorting

Data can be sorted in Microsoft® Access database or a Microsoft® Excel spreadsheet in the following order:

Alphabetical or alphanumeric data – ascending order (A-Z)
Apple
Banana
Cherry
Grapefruit
Pear
Water melon

Alphabetical or alphanumeric data – descending order (Z-A)
Water melon
Pear
Grapefruit
Cherry
Banana
Apple

Text is aligned to the left of a cell

Numerical data – ascending order Smallest to largest
1
4
6
10
15
20

Numerical data – descending order Largest to smallest
20
15
10
6
4
1

Numbers and dates are aligned to the right of a cell

Chronological data – ascending order Least recent to most recent
01/01/2001
31/12/2001
01/01/2004
31/12/2005
20/01/2006
21/06/2010

Chronological data – descending order Most recent to least recent
21/06/2010
20/01/2006
31/12/2005
01/01/2004
31/12/2001
01/01/2001

Searching

Data within a Microsoft® Access database or a Microsoft® Excel spreadsheet can be filtered to find specified information. For example, a retail company may want to target their advertising in a specific location or area. To do this, the customer records can be filtered (in both a spreadsheet and database) or queried (database only) to find only the chosen location (e.g. Chester or London).

A filter or query is created using *search criteria*. The search criteria *Chester* or *London* would be entered beneath the correct field name (e.g. **City**). The filter or query results will show only records which include the specified location.

Both filters and queries use comparison and logical operators to find information. See some examples below:

Comparison Operators
= equal to (e.g. =Chester would find all records which include this city)
> greater than (e.g. >50, will find all records which contain numbers greater than 50) **>= greater than or equal to** (e.g. >=50 will find all records which contain numbers of 50 and above)
< less than   (e.g. <50 will find all records which contain numbers less than this figure) **<= less than or equal to**   (e.g. <=50 will find all records which contain numbers of 50 and below

Logical Operators
OR Example: Chester OR London (to find records that contain both Chester and London)
AND Example: >=01/01/2010 AND <=31/12/2010 To find dates in 2010
NOT Example: Chester NOT London To find records which contain Chester but exclude London

 © Lorna Bointon, Qualiteach Education 2010

Help Sheets

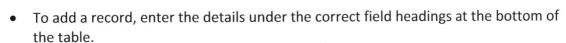

To find out how to do it, follow the instructions below

Enter and edit data

Table Datasheet

- To add a record, enter the details under the correct field headings at the bottom of the table.

- Data can be edited by adding records, deleting records and editing fields.

- To amend a field, click into the field and make the changes. Click away from the record to save the changes.

- To delete a record, select the record and then press the **Delete** key on the keyboard. Confirm the deletion when prompted.

Spreadsheet

- Click into a cell and type in the data, pressing Enter or one of the directional arrow keys on the keyboard or clicking the tick on the Formula Bar when complete.

- Data can be edited within a cell by double clicking the cell and then editing as required.

- To delete rows or columns, select the row/column and then, from the **Home** tab and **Cells** group, select the **Delete** arrow. Choose **Delete Sheet Rows** or **Delete Sheet Columns**.

- To insert rows/columns select the row/column and then, from the **Home** tab and **Cells** group, select the **Insert** arrow. Choose **Insert Sheet Rows** or **Insert Sheet Columns**.

Sorting – Microsoft® Access

- Select the column/field to be sorted and then click the required sort button from the **Home** tab and the **Sort & Filter** group.

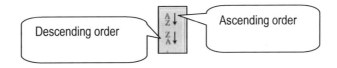

Descending order   Ascending order

Queries – Microsoft® Access

- Select the **Create** tab and then select the **Query Design** button. Select the table in which you want to search for data and click **Add**. Click **Close**.

Query Design

- Double click each of the fields to display them in the **Field** row of the **Query** grid

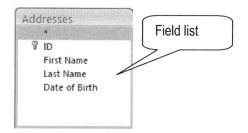

- Enter the criteria into the **Criteria** field beneath the relevant field heading (e.g. enter Mason under the **Last Name** field to find all records containing that surname)

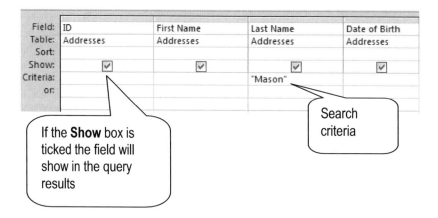

- Select the **Show** tick box to show fields or de-select the Show box to hide fields in the query results

- To sort a query, click the **Sort** arrow beneath the appropriate field name and then select a sort order (ascending or descending)

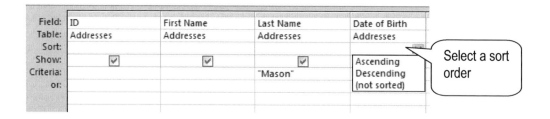

- To see the query results, select the **Run** button

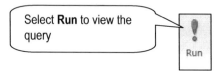

Simple Filters – Microsoft® Access

- Select the appropriate field and then, from the **Home** tab and the **Sort & Filter** group, select the **Filter** button

- Select the criteria and click **OK** or, if filtering numerical data, select the **Number Filters** sub-menu and if filtering text, select the **Text Filters** sub-menu. Choose a comparison operator (such as > greater than etc)

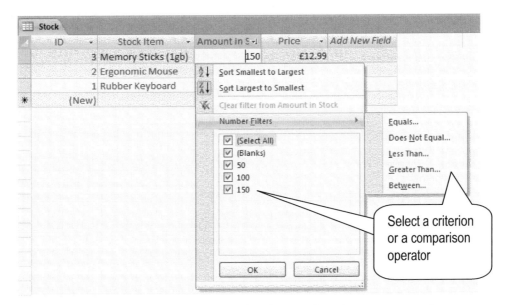

- The **Custom Filter** dialog box appears displaying the chosen comparison operator and a box in which to enter the criteria.

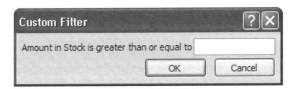

Advanced Filters – Microsoft® Access

- Select the appropriate field and then, from the **Home** tab and the **Sort &** Filter group, select the **Advanced** button. Select **Advanced Filter/Sort**.

- Enter the field headings into the grid.

- Enter the criteria beneath the relevant field heading.

- To apply the filter, select the **Advanced** button and then select **Apply Filter/Sort** from the menu.

- To save the filter as a query, select the **Advanced** button and then select **Save as Query** from the menu. Type in a name and click **OK**.

Toggle Filter (turn on/off)

- From the **Home** tab and the **Sort & Filter** group, select the **Toggle Filter** button to switch between filtered and unfiltered data.

Filters – Microsoft® Excel

- Select (highlight) the spreadsheet data. Select the **Data** tab and then, from the **Sort & Filter** group, click the **Filter** command.

- The spreadsheet data will display filter arrows in the field heading of each field. Click a filter arrow to select criteria by which to filter the information.

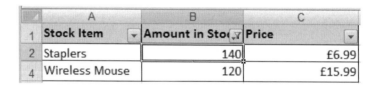

- Select a criteria or click the **Number** or **Text Filters** sub-menu to see a sub-menu displaying comparison operators:

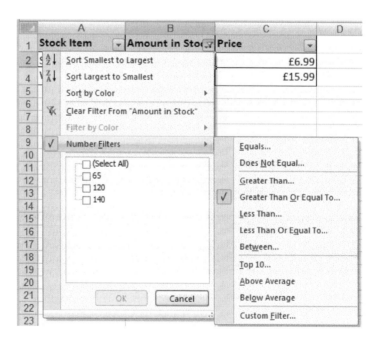

- The **Custom Filter** dialog box will appear displaying the chosen comparison operator and boxes in which to enter the criteria.

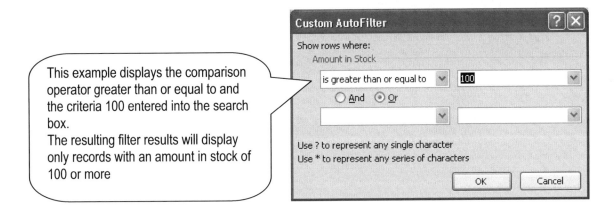

This example displays the comparison operator greater than or equal to and the criteria 100 entered into the search box.
The resulting filter results will display only records with an amount in stock of 100 or more

- Re-select the **Filter** button to switch between filtered and unfiltered data.

Sorting – Microsoft® Excel

- To sort data in a spreadsheet table, select the data and then select the **Sort** buttons from the **Data** tab. Select **A to Z** (ascending or largest to smallest) or **Z to A** (descending or smallest to largest):

Sort in ascending order

Sort in descending order

Show or Hide Fields

- Select the column to be hidden in the filter results and then, from the **Home** tab and the **Cells** group, select the **Format** button.

- From the **Format** menu, select **Hide & Unhide** and then select **Hide Columns**. To unhide columns, re-select the **Format** menu and select **Unhide Columns**.

Match Makers

Match the correct answers with the questions below:

1.	Dates are sorted in this order?	a.	Alphabetical
2.	Text is sorted in this order?	b.	Descending
3.	Numbers are sorted in this order?	c.	Chronological
4.	This order displays dates from most recent to least recent?	d.	Numerical

Enter your answers below:

1.		2.		3.		4.	

As Easy As....

1.   Which of the following searches would find records that contain Bradford or Leeds?

A	Bradford and Leeds	☐
B	=Bradford	☐
C	Bradford not Leeds	☐
D	Bradford or Leeds	☐

2.   Which of the following search criteria would be successful in finding records which contain items that cost £35 or more?

A	>35	☐
B	<=35	☐
C	>=35	☐
D	<35	☐

Practical Exercise 1

1. Open the database called **Friends.accdb** in Microsoft® Access.

2. Enter the following data to the **Birthdays** table:

First Name	Last Name	Date of Birth
Sarah	Mason	11/11/1995
Robert	Mason	03/02/1994
John	Connor	12/04/1996
Brendan	Carter	10/10/1996
Gill	Tarrant	12/03/1994

3. Make the following amendments to the data in the **Birthdays** table:

Change Gill's first name to Jill

Change Robert's date of birth to 05/02/1994

Delete the record for Brendan Carter

Add the following new record: **Hannah Browne, 13/01/1995**

4. Save and close the table and the **Friends** database.

Practical Exercise 2

1. Open the database called **Sales.accdb** in Microsoft® Access.

2. Enter the following data to the **Stock** table:

Stock Item	Amount in Stock	Price
Rubber Keyboard	50	£14.99
Ergonomic Mouse	100	£35.99
Memory Sticks (1gb)	150	£12.99

3. Save and close the table and the **Sales** database.

Practical Exercise 3

1.   Open **Friends.accdb** and the **Birthdays** table.

2.   Sort the Date of Birth field in ascending order (least recent to most recent).

3.   Query the data to find records with the Last Name **Mason.**

4.   Save the query as **LastName** and close.

5.   Close the **Friends** database.

Practical Exercise 4

1.   Open **Sales.accdb** and the **Stock** table.

2.   Sort the Amount in Stock field in descending order (largest to smallest).

3.   Filter the data to find only records that contain stock items with 60 or more in stock.

4.   Remove the filter.

5.   Filter the data to find prices higher than £20.

6.   Remove the filter.

7.   Close the **Sales** database.

Practical Exercise 5

1.   Open Microsoft® Excel and a new spreadsheet. Save the spreadsheet as **New_stock.**

2.   Enter the data below and resave the spreadsheet:

Stock Item	Amount in Stock	Price
Mouse mats	65	£9.99
Wireless Mouse	120	£15.99
Staplers	140	£6.99

3.   Sort the data in ascending order of Price.

4.   Filter the data to find only records which contain 100 or more items in stock (2 items).

5.   Save and close the spreadsheet.

Section 9 ▶

Developing, Presenting and Communicating
Information

Mail

Use communications software to meet the requirements of a straightforward task

Use E-mail

An email is a means of communication via electronic mail which can be sent and received via a computer with an Internet connection, a phone line and a modem.

An Internet Service Provider (ISP) provides connectivity for a fee. There are many ISPs available from which to choose, each with varying costs and services.

Broadband connection enables a user to send and receive email messages without preventing telephone calls from being made or received. Dial-up, although cheaper because the user only pays when they use the service, prevents usage of the telephone line whilst the user is online.

Email messages can be managed through applications, such as Outlook Express or Outlook 2007. Alternatively, email can also be managed via webmail accounts such as hotmail (e.g. accessing email through the Internet rather than a software application). Webmail can be accessed from any computer, anywhere in the world where an Internet connection is available.

WIFI hotspots provide Internet connectivity via portable and mobile devices, such as laptops, mobile phones etc, and can be found in many areas such as shopping centres, airports and restaurants, motels. Hotspots can be located through searches via a search engine, such as Google hotspot finder.

A user can send a new message to one or more recipients (a recipient is someone who receives), reply to a message and forward messages. Attachments are files which are attached to an email message. For example, holiday photographs can be sent to friends as attachments in an email. A subject should be added to a message so the recipient can see what the email is about before opening it. Be careful about using bad language in an email as this can result in users being banned from email forums and chat rooms.

Be careful about opening emails and attachments from senders that you do not know. They may contain viruses or other threats that can be downloaded onto your computer or spread to other users via email.

Email addresses are entered into the **To:** field and separated by a semicolon (;). An example of an email address is **contact@qualiteach.co.uk**. The first part of an email address is the *username* followed by the @ (at) symbol. The next part of the address is called the *domain name*, which sometimes includes the geographical location (UK)

Email addresses can be stored as contacts. A list of contacts is called a distribution list.

Use appropriate language with different recipients. For example, the tone and language style used to chat with a friend will be different to the tone and language used in a business email.

Other types of communication include *blogs* (web blogs) which are online diaries, *wikis* which can be edited directly from a user's browser and online forums and chat rooms which allow users to chat and keep in contact in 'real time'.

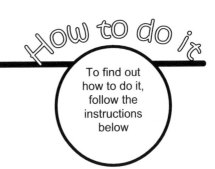

To find out how to do it, follow the instructions below

Outlook Express

Read an E-mail

- The **Inbox** displays received messages. If the message is displayed in **Bold** it is unread. To open a message double click it or right click the message and select **Open**

Create and Send an E-mail

- To create a new email message, select the **Create mail** button. Enter the email address or addresses (separated by a semi colon) in the **To** field or to send a copy of the message to another recipient, add the address or addresses to the **CC** field. Enter the address or addresses into the **BCC** field if you don't want the other recipients of the message to see their address. Enter a subject for the message in the **Subject** box. Enter text into the message area. Click the **Send** button.

Reply to an email

- Received messages are displayed in the Inbox. Select the message to which you want to reply and then select the **Reply** button (the **Reply All** button will send a reply to all of the recipients of the original email). The original sender's email address will be displayed in the **To** field. Enter your text at the top of the message, above the original message details (To, From, Date etc). Click the **Send** button.

Forward an email

- Select the message that you want to forward to another recipient. Click the **Forward** button. Enter the email address or addresses in the **To:** field, separating addresses with a semi colon. Add an address or addresses to the **CC** field if you want to send a copy to that address. Enter an address or addresses into the **BCC** field if you don't want the other recipients of the message to see it. Enter your text above the original message details (To, From, Date etc). Click the **Send** button.

Attach a file to an E-mail message

- Click the **Attach (**paperclip**)** button or select the **Insert** menu and then **File Attachment**. Find and select the file to be attached and then click the **Attach** button. The file will display in the **Attach** box.

Open and Save Attachments

- Open the message containing the attached files. Double click a file attachment to open it or right click and select **Open**. For some files, the **Mail Attachment** dialog box will open. Click the **Open** button to confirm that you want to open the file or click **Cancel** to abort the operation. To save an attachment, open the message, right click the attached file and select **Save As**. Select the correct drive/folder in which to save the file and click **Save.**

- The example below displays a new message addressed to Hannah and Brendan and copied to another recipient (Briony). To keep an email address confidential and private from the other recipients it should be entered in the BCC field. The attached file, Party Poster.docx, appears in the Attach field:

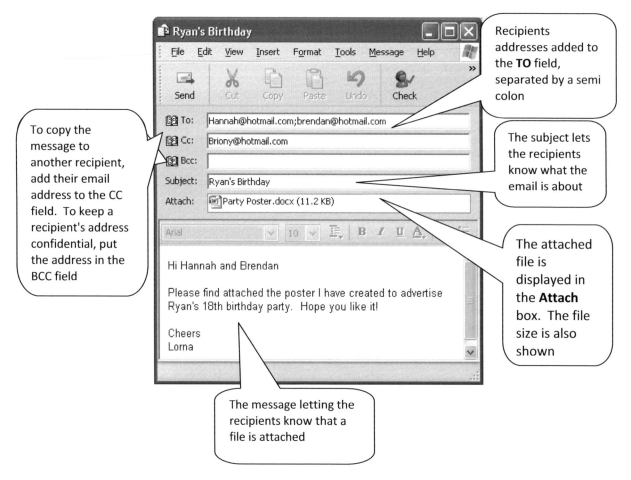

Delete an email

- Select the message to be deleted by left clicking once. Press the **Delete** key on the keyboard or click the **Delete** button on the toolbar. The deleted message will be stored in the **Deleted Items** folder, from which it can be retrieved or permanently deleted.

Contacts

Create a Contact:

- Open an email message and right click the sender's email address. Select **Add to Contacts**. Alternatively, select the **File** menu and then click **New Contact**. Enter details for the contact and click **OK**.

Create a Contact/Distribution List:

- Select the **Addresses** button. Select the **New** button and then select **New Group** from the menu. Type in a group name for the contacts list. Click the **Select Members** button. Select the contacts that you want to include in the contacts list and then click the **Select** button. Repeat to add all contacts to the list. Click **OK**.

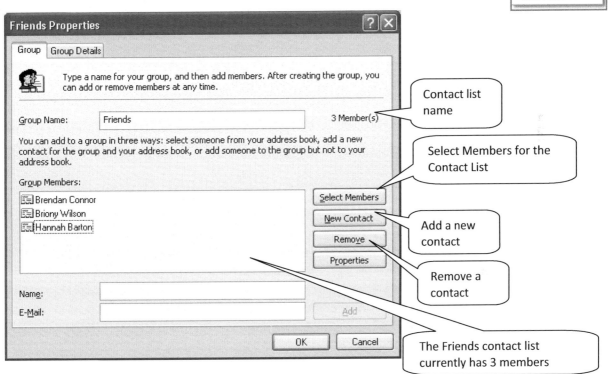

Edit or Delete a Contact:

- *Edit:* Click the **Addresses** button. From the **Address Book** right click the contact to be edited and select **Properties**. Select the appropriate tab (e.g. Name) and make the necessary changes. Select **Edit** to edit the email address or **Remove** to remove the email address.
- *Delete:* Click the **Addresses** button or click a contact from the list of contacts in the Inbox (bottom left of screen, beneath Folders). Right click the contact and then select **Delete**. Click **Yes** to confirm deletion.

Add a Contacts List to an Email Message:

- Open a new message and select the **To** field. Select the contact list name and click the **To** button. Repeat to add other contacts to the **CC** or **BCC** fields. Click OK.

9.1 Activities

Have a Go

Try the activities below to test yourself on the previous section

Match Makers

Match the correct answers with the questions below:

1.	A stored email address?	a.	Username
2.	A list of stored addresses?	b.	Contact
3.	The first part of an email addresses displayed before the @ symbol is called a?	c.	Domain name
4.	The part of an email address displayed after the @ symbol is called ?	d.	Distribution list

Enter your answers below:

1.		2.		3.		4.	

As Easy As....

1. A wireless Internet connection available to use with mobile devices?

A	WIKI	☐
B	ISP	☐
C	URL	☐
D	WIFI	☐

2. What is a blog?

A	An online discussion forum	☐
B	A podcast	☐
C	A web log or online diary	☐
D	A chat room enabling 'real time' chat	☐

Practical Exercise 1

1.   Create a new email message and enter your own email address in the **To:** field

2.   Enter a friend's email address in the **CC:** field (let them know what you are doing and ask their permission first)

3.   Add **Functional Skills ICT** as the subject

4.   Enter the following text in the message area:

> Hi *(add friend's name here)*
>
> I've attached one of the files that I have created as part of the Functional Skills ICT Level 1 course.
>
> Regards
>
> *Add your name*

5.   Attach a file that you have created from a previous exercise, such as **Format.docx** (don't attach a database file as some email applications will not accept messages with databases attached). Send the message.

Practical Exercise 2

1.   Open the message that you have just sent to your own email address and save the attached file. If a message appears to let you know that the file already exists and asking if you want to replace it, click **Yes.**

Practical Exercise 3

1.   Create a contacts list called **Friends** with the following addresses:

Hannah Barton

Brendan Connor

Briony Wilson

2.   Create a new message and add the Friends contact list to the **To** field. Enter the subject **Ryan's Party** and the message text: **Hope you can come to Ryan's 18th Birthday Party!** Send the message.

Stay Safe and Respect Others

Did You Know?

BCC in an email message stands for Blind Carbon Copy

Confidentiality

To ensure the confidentiality of an email address, enter it in the **BCC** field (blind carbon copy) and the address will be hidden from other recipients of the same email message.

Before sending a message or photographs to recipients in a contacts list, think about whether it is appropriate to send it to each of the recipients in the contact list. Some of the recipients may not know each other and may not want others to see their photos or email address or other details.   Ask permission before sending photographs of people to other recipients or posting on a website.

Respect Others

Always use appropriate language when communicating on a social networking group or chat room/forum. Be careful not to use inflammatory or bad language or be insulting or disrespectful to others. Using bad language or language designed to make people angry is called **flaming** and can get a user banned from online forums. Be careful to respect the views of other people and be tolerant towards gender, age or cultural differences. Always ask permission before communicating another person's views or opinions.

Stay Safe

It has become increasingly important to take care of personal details since the advent of social networking sites (a social networking site is a site, such as Twitter or Facebook, where a user posts details about themselves and allows other people to communicate with them via instant messaging and email).

Users of social networking sites should be careful about what information they post about themselves and others. Always ask permission before posting any information or photos of other people. To prevent identity theft and fraudulent use of your personal details, it is good practice to limit the people who can view your personal details to specific friends and family members. To avoid the possibility of a stranger using your details for fraudulent purposes, you should never provide the following information on a social networking site:

- Your address
- Your date of birth
- Photographs containing you or friends
- Telephone number
- Email address

Match Makers

Match the correct answers with the questions below:

| 1. | Language used in forums or chat rooms which is designed to provoke and make people angry | a. | Hides email addresses |

| 2. | Blind Carbon Copy is used for this purpose? | b. | Flaming |

| 3. | Posting your personal details online may result in? | c. | Social networks |

| 4. | Twitter and Facebook are examples of? | d. | Identity theft |

Enter your answers below:

| 1. | | 2. | | 3. | | 4. | |

As Easy As....

1. Why should you add an email address to the BCC field in an email message?

A	To ensure that other recipient's see it	☐
B	To ensure that other recipients don't see it	☐
C	To ensure recipients privacy in the **To:** field	☐
D	To ensure recipients privacy in the **CC:** field	☐

2. What should you do before posting a photograph of friends on a website?

A	Ask each of your friends for permission before posting the photo	☐
B	Post the photo but don't add their names	☐
C	Post the photo after gaining permission from only one of your friends	☐
D	Post the photo and let them know afterwards	☐

Section 10 ▸

Developing, Presenting and Communicating
Information

View

Combine information within a publication for a familiar audience and purpose

Output

Did You Know?

DPI stands for dots per inch, the more DPI the better the quality

Combine Information

Information can be combined for a variety of purposes, such as:

- A poster advertising a birthday party combining text, Word Art and pictures
- A presentation combining text, pictures, charts and spreadsheets
- A report combining text with analytical or statistical data or graphs from a spreadsheet
- An information sheet combining text, charts and images or a table of prices
- A webpage containing text, video, animations, audio and images

Printing

The output of combined information depends on whether it will be viewed as a printout (hard copy) or on-screen such as in a web page.

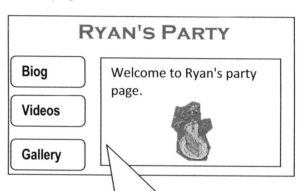

Poster and web page combining text and images. Reports - combining text/table and text/chart

Ryan's Party Budget Report	
Ryan's birthday party arrangements include venue, entertainment, catering and postage.	The total costs must not exceed £800. The costs below need to be confirmed.

Ryan's 18th Birthday Party	
Venue	£150.00
Catering	£350.00
Entertainment	£250.00
Postal costs	£10.00
Total Costs	**£760.00**

Ryan's Party Budget Report	
Ryan's birthday party arrangements include venue, entertainment, catering and postage.	The total costs must not exceed £800. The costs below need to be confirmed.

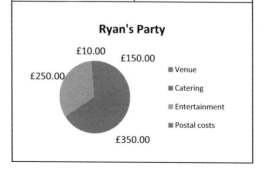

How to do it

To find out how to do it, follow the instructions below

Combining Information

For help on inserting images and tables, see section 7.1.

Switch between open windows

- Open files will display as tabs on the task bar. Click a tab to open the file. Alternatively, select the **View** tab and then click **Switch Windows**. Choose the file to open.
- **Tip:** A shortcut key combination for switching between windows is **Alt** and **Tab**.

Insert graphs/spreadsheet data using copy and paste

- Open Excel and the file containing the graph/data. Select the graph or spreadsheet data to be copied and click the **Copy** button from the **Clipboard** group.
- Switch to the open document and select **Paste**.

Insert movies and sounds in MS PowerPoint

Movie clips:
- Select the **Insert** tab and then, from the **Movie Clips** group, click **Movie**.
- Select Movie from File.

- Locate the movie file and click **OK**. A message will appear asking you to select how you want the movie to start in the slide show – **Automatically** or **When Clicked** – click an option to insert the movie into the slide show.
- Movies can also be inserted from the Clip Organiser. Select this option from the Movie menu, and then choose a movie clip from the task pane.

Sound files
- Select the **Insert** tab and then, from the **Movie Clips** group, click **Sound**.
- Select **Sound from File** if it is saved on your computer, or select from **Clip Organiser** to insert a sound from the Clipart gallery.
- Locate the sound file and click **OK**. A message will appear asking you to select how you want the sound to start in the slide show – **Automatically** or **When Clicked** – click an option to insert the sound file into the slide show.

Checking Techniques

Proofreading

It is important to ensure that a finished publication or document is free from errors. Mistakes appear unprofessional and can detract from the intended message being conveyed within the document.

Proofreading means checking every word carefully to ensure that text is accurate and that meaning is clear. Proofreading also covers layout and presentation of a document and ensures that the language style is appropriate. Proofreading literary work is performed by book editors/publishers and proofreading agencies.

Check layout and style

The layout of a document should be appropriate for the information or message it is trying to convey and should be suited to the correct age group, gender or specific interest of the reader. For example, a poster for a party will use a different layout and style to a formal business letter.

Check for meaning

The meaning of information within a document or publication should be clear and free from bias or prejudice. It is important that text and images are checked to ensure that the meaning is being conveyed correctly.

Spell Check

Each of the Microsoft® Office applications contains a spelling tool which will check text for accuracy. When a spelling error is found, it is displayed in the Spelling dialog box with suggestions for correct spellings. Be careful about relying entirely on the Spelling tool and proofread text carefully. The Spell Check facility will display words that are not in its dictionary as errors, such as proper nouns, e.g. first and last names, and scientific words. Some spelling errors may not be identified if the spelling matches another word – for example, typing 'to' instead of 'too' (**to** is a correct word but if used in the wrong context instead of **too** it will not be identified as a spelling error – for example, *'It was to much'*).

Preview

To ensure that the layout and page structure is correct and appropriate for the type of information it contains, the document or publication should be previewed before printing. Previewing work before printing ensures that paper wastage is kept to a minimum and ensures professional output.

> **Tip:** To learn how to use the spelling tool and print preview, see **Help Sheets 7.1a.**

Activities

Match Makers

Match the correct answers with the questions below:

1.	Use this to view layout and page structure?	a.	Proofreading

2.	Use this to find and correct typing errors?	b.	Print preview

3.	This checking technique is used by editors and book publishers to ensure accuracy?	c.	Meaning

4.	To ensure that the correct message is conveyed, the information should be checked for......... ?	d.	Spell Check

Enter your answers below:

1.		2.		3.		4.	

As Easy As....

A B C

1.   Which of the following does not combine information?

A	A poster with text and images	☐
B	A report with text and charts	☐
C	A presentation with text, images and video	☐
D	A business letter to a customer	☐

2.   DPI stands for which of the following?

A	Dots per inch	☐
B	Dots per image	☐
C	Display per image	☐
D	Display picture image	☐

Practical Exercise 1

1. Create a new document and enter the following text including the deliberate spelling errors:

> Combinning information within an publication involves combining text with immages, charts and tabels.

2. Use a combination of proof reading and spell checking to check and correct the text that you have just entered (tip: there are three spelling errors and one grammatical error which proof reading should identify).

3. Save the document as **combine.docx.**

Practical Exercise 2

1. Continue using **combine.docx.** Using Clip Art, insert an image of your choice and apply wrapping so that the image wraps to the right of the text. Resize the image as appropriate.

2. Beneath the text, copy and paste the pie chart from the **party** spreadsheet that you created in a previous exercise. Resize the chart as appropriate.

3. Resave the **combine** document and close.

Practical Exercise 3

1. Create a new presentation. The first slide should be a Title and Content slide with the heading **Audio.**

2. Insert the **Telephone** sound file from Clip Art beneath the heading. Ensure that it will start automatically.

3. The second slide should be a Title and Content slide with the heading **Movie Clips.**

4. Insert a movie clip of your choice from Clip Art beneath the heading.

5. The third slide should be a Title and Content slide with the heading **Charts.**

6. Insert the pie chart that you created in a previous exercise beneath the heading.

7. Save the presentation as **Objects.pptx** and close.

Section 11 ▶

Developing, Presenting and Communicating
Information

Judge

Evaluate own use of ICT tools

Evaluation Techniques

What is Evaluation?

Evaluation means reviewing the usefulness of ICT tools that have been used to complete a task.

This may require considering whether other ICT tools could have completed the task more quickly or easily.

Evaluation should be completed at each stage of a task and also at the task's completion to ensure that ICT tools effectively achieve the desired result.

Factors to consider:

There are many ICT tools which can be used to create, develop and present information in a variety of different formats. It is important to think about how the information will be displayed e.g. as printed output or viewed on screen.

Other considerations are:

- Duration – how long has it taken to complete the task using the chosen ICT tools. Could the task be completed using less time and money with different ICT tools?

- Different file formats - consider whether some files may need to be saved in a different file format or software version so that other users can access them.

- Results – could you have achieved better results using different software packages and tools?

- Downloading – think about length of time taken to download large file sizes. Could smaller file sizes be achieved by saving files in other file formats? Consider the speed of an internet connection and whether this could be an issue when downloading files from a web page.

An evaluation sheet should contain the following:

- Type of task e.g. presentation
- The ICT tools used to complete the task e.g. Microsoft® PowerPoint
- Actions taken to ensure that the result is fit for purpose, e.g. proofreading, checking layout, format and accuracy
- A consideration of what worked and what didn't work so well, e.g. did the digital (sound/video) content make the presentation more exciting or more distracting?

Have a Go

Try the activities below to test yourself on the previous section

Match Makers

Match the correct answers with the questions below:

1.	These are important when downloading files?	a.	Software version
2.	This can affect costs and deadlines	b.	File sizes
3.	Connection speeds can affect this?	c.	Task duration
4.	Saving in this format helps another user to access the file using older software?	d.	Downloading Internet files

Enter your answers below:

1.		2.		3.		4.	

As Easy As....

1. When should evaluation take place?

A	Once the task is completed	☐
B	At each stage of a task so that it doesn't have to be performed at the end	☐
C	At each stage in the task and at completion	☐
D	At the beginning of the task	☐

2. What is meant by the term 'ICT Tools'

A	Screwdrivers and other small tools to work on computer components	☐
B	Software tools and commands	☐
C	The means to operate a computer through use of hardware, e.g. keyboard, mouse etc	☐
D	Peripherals such as the printer or scanner	☐

Answers ▶

Mark

Answers to Section Activities

1.1 Activities

Match Makers

1.	C	2.	D	3.	B	4.	A

1. Before starting a task it is important to **PLAN** it thoroughly beforehand

2. To ensure that a task is completed on time it is important to work to a **TIMESCALE**

3. A **STORYBOARD** is a rough design or initial plan

4. A **MIND MAP** is a visual way of showing the thought processes involved in planning a project

5. A **SPREADSHEET** can help you work out costs of a task or project

As Easy As

1C, 2A, 3A, 4D

2.1 Activities

Match Makers

1.	B	2.	F	3.	A	4.	C	5.	G	6.	D	7.	E

As Easy As

1B, 2D, 3A, 4A

2.2 Activities

Match Makers

1.	B	2.	D	3.	A	4.	C

As Easy As

1C, 2A, 3C, 4A, 5B

2.3 Activities

Match Makers

1.	D	2.	C	3.	A	4.	B

As Easy As

1C

3.1 Activities

Match Makers

1.	D	2.	A	3.	B	4.	C

As Easy As

1A

4.1 Activities

Match Makers

1.	D	2.	C	3.	A	4.	B

As Easy As

1B

4.2 Activities

Match Makers

1.	D	2.	A	3.	D	4.	B

As Easy As

1A

5.1 Activities

Match Makers

1.	B	2.	D	3.	A	4.	C

As Easy As

1D

5.2 Activities

Match Makers

1.	C	2.	D	3.	A	4.	B

As Easy As

1C

6.1 Activities

Match Makers

1.	B	2.	D	3.	A	4.	C

As Easy As

1D, 2A

7.1a Activities

Match Makers

1.	B	2.	A	3.	D	4.	C

As Easy As

1C, 2A

7.1b Activities

Match Makers

1.	B	2.	C	3.	D	4.	A

As Easy As

1A, 2B

7.1c Activities

Match Makers

1.	B	2.	A	3.	D	4.	C

As Easy As

1B, 2D

7.1d Activities

Match Makers

1.	B	2.	C	3.	D	4.	A

As Easy As

1B, 2B

8.1 Activities

Match Makers

1.	C	2.	A	3.	D	4.	B

As Easy As

1D, 2A

8.2 Activities

Match Makers

1.	C	2.	A	3.	D	4.	B

As Easy As

1A, 2B

8.3 Activities

Match Makers

1.	C	2.	D	3.	A	4.	B

As Easy As

1C, 2A

8.4 Activities

Match Makers

1.	C	2.	A	3.	D	4.	B

As Easy As

1D, 2C

9.1 Activities

Match Makers

1.	B	2.	D	3.	A	4.	C

As Easy As

1A, 2C

9.2 Activities

Match Makers

1.	B	2.	A	3.	D	4.	C

As Easy As

1B, 2A

10.1/10.2 Activities

Match Makers

1.	B	2.	D	3.	A	4.	C

As Easy As

1D, 2A

11.1 Activities

Match Makers

1.	B	2.	C	3.	D	4.	A

As Easy As

1C, 2B